# The Beyond Within

*The Downtown Dao of Lan Su Chinese Garden*

ALSO BY DANIEL SKACH-MILLS

*The Tao of Now*
*The Hut Beneath the Pine: Tea Poems*
*In This Forest of Monks*
*Manzou*

# The Beyond Within

*The Downtown Dao of Lan Su Chinese Garden*

by
Daniel Skach-Mills
(Dan Daoren)

The Beyond Within
*The Downtown Dao of Lan Su Chinese Garden*
by Daniel Skach-Mills
©Copyright 2017 by Daniel Skach-Mills
skachmills@gmail.com
Design by Dan Lucas
Cover photograph by Dan Huynh
Illustrations by Lu Kesi
Cover chop seal design by Lu Kesi
Seal translation: "Dan Daoren" or "Dao Man Dan"
Author photograph courtesy of Margaret Chula
ISBN 978-0-692-83818-1

*This book is dedicated to*
*my great-aunt, Yvonne Bourgeois;*
*and to Zetta Schneider,*
*whose yard was a wonderland of flowers and streams.*
*Your lives were gardens for me.*

*And*

*in fond memory of Sam Dresselhaus*
*(1977–2014)*
*who listened to the fragrance.*

# Contents

*Look and you will see how each form, each thing longs*
*to be unencumbered by externals and to dwell again in the Beyond*
*which we embody and ripen within ourselves.*

*– Rainer Maria Rilke*

After giving one of my tours at Lan Su Chinese Garden in Portland, Oregon, a woman approached me and asked, "So what keeps bringing you back to give tours here after all these years? What is it about this place that speaks to you?" Without so much as a pause I responded, "The garden is my true face."

My answer was like nothing I could have thought up or anticipated. It surprised me as much as it probably did her. But isn't that what the universe is in love with—surprise?

What did your face look like before you were born? This is a *koan*, or riddle, that a Chan (in Japanese it's Zen) Buddhist master might ask a student in order to bring about a moment of spiritual awakening or enlightenment. Designed to bypass your thinking mind, a *koan* cannot be answered intellectually. It demands an unconditioned and spontaneous response that can only come when the student has experientially glimpsed his or her real or "true" face— the face that has been there since before the beginning of time; the changeless face that lives within, beyond all the personal and cultural masks we sculpt from beliefs, ideas, and opinions, possessions, careers, and roles.

*I'm talking about your real face,*
*the one before Clinique,*
*and Max Factor, and skin.*

*Look at you,*
*always making up who you are*
*out of that ridiculously tiny compact!*

*If only you could see*
*the vastness of your own truth*
*reflected between these words.*

*No mirror would ever*
*be large enough.*

What does the Beyond Within mean? What's it pointing to? To me, it reveals the paradox that only by looking within yourself can you begin to see beyond what you think of as yourself. And no one can do this for you. A sage can point to the path, but you must walk it. The Internet can provide information, but you can't Google your inner life. Look even deeper and you'll discover this paradox works both ways. Looking within you see what's beyond yourself; looking beyond you see what's within yourself. This realization turns the garden into a mirror in which you can glimpse the natural world and the ineffable mystery that underlies it *as your own reflection*, your true face. Or, as a Chan master once said when asked to describe enlightenment, "The universe is my true personality."

Throughout history, many spiritual teachers have taught that what appears to lie beyond us is, in fact, waiting to manifest within us as who and what we truly are. Jesus said, "The kingdom of heaven is within you." The Buddha taught that within each of us there's an unsullied center of sanity, wisdom, and goodness. He called this center our original nature. The twelfth century Sufi poet, Rumi, confides that he spent years knocking at the spiritual door, only to discover he'd been knocking from inside. The Wiccan spiritual tradition describes it yet another way: "As above, so below. As within, so without. As the universe, so the soul." And in Daoism (pronounced: "dow-ism," although often spelled "Taoism") Laozi's words from the *Daodejing* still echo the truth across millennia: "Without looking out your window, you can realize the eternal Dao."

What these teachings seem to point to is that the universe and the supreme reality or mystery at the heart of all existence aren't somewhere *out there*. Yes, Laozi did say, "The journey of a thousand miles begins with a single step." But the spiritual miles we trek can increase by who-knows-how-many thousands or tens-of-thousands the more we let thinking separate heaven from earth, and divinity from our humanity. Unwittingly, we can fall into the trap of becoming lifelong spiritual pilgrims or seekers forever on the way, forever striving to arrive where we already are. "You are that which you are seeking" are the words St. Francis of Assisi used centuries ago in an attempt to stop us in our peregrinating tracks.

*You've seen the sky outside,*
*but have you beheld the sky inside?*

*You've gazed out of thousands of windows*
*at the world that lies beyond,*
*but have you once peered within*
*at what lies beyond the world?*

*For years now*
*just look at how blind I've been,*
*stumbling repeatedly over the Divine*
*in the dim light of words!*
*searching frantically*
*for the doorway*
*in a wall-less room!*

*From this moment on*
*let me be a candle lit only by darkness;*
*a key that's locked itself forever*
*out of inner and outer,*
*open or closed.*

*You can't Google your inner life.*

For a Daoist, heaven wasn't some invisible, metaphysical place you had to physically die to enter. As Confucius' grandson Zisi (450 BCE) wrote, "Nothing is more obvious than the hidden. Nothing is more visible than the unseen." To the awakened eye and heart, heaven could be experienced here and now as a felt unity with life, landscapes, and the natural forces shaping them. Mountains radiated this energetic union, rising up to join temporal and celestial together into a sacred and unified universe.

Throughout my life I've been attracted to places that emanate this numinous energy (*ling qi*). These have included a Benedictine and a Trappist monastery; the city of Nelson, nestled in the Selkirk mountains of British Columbia in Canada; the alpine village of Zermatt, home of the Matterhorn in Switzerland; and Portland's Lan Su Chinese Garden to name just a few.

In some indescribable way, these settings reflected back to me my innermost self, my deep inner terrain. Garden, monastery, mountains—my initial encounter with each one felt somehow familiar to me. It's as if who and what I truly am on the inside recognized itself in what appeared to be outside, resulting in a felt reverberation, attraction, or pull. Some might call this an experience of wonder, which we'll touch on later. The closest I can come to describing my experience is that I awakened to these places as myself. I woke up to the Beyond within.

*We say we live in a place—*
*but don't the places we love*
*also live in us?*

*We yearn for what's eternal—*
*but how could we long for it*
*unless it were already here?*

*Ji Cheng said: "To learn*
*the art of enjoying your life*
*is to become an Immortal."*

*The heart is the long road back*
*to where you've always*
*been standing.*

Often, after a tour, someone will ask, "Have you written down what you shared with us today? Where can I read more?" This book is my response to these requests. It's an expanded version of my tour that you can use as a guide—both to the garden, and to the Beyond within yourself.

Obviously, there simply isn't time for me to go in-depth about the garden on a forty-five minute guided tour. As a docent, what I try to give visitors is an overview of five key elements that make up a Chinese garden, and how those elements, together with spiritual and philosophical principles, work together to make such a garden not only the Beverly Hills mansion of its day, but a truly sacred space.

To remain consistent with my tour, I focus here on these elements: water, rock, architecture, poetry, and plants. I then couple each one with a Daoist principle that seems to naturally and organically complement the element in some meaningful way.

Furthermore, I wish to state up front that I have no academic credentials in Chinese history, language, or culture. (As of this writing, I've never been to China, although I must say I feel like I experience everything that makes China what it is every time I step through the garden gate.) As such, any scholarly information you find here has been gleaned and synthesized over the years from a variety of sources based on personal reading and study. I also want to point out that the views expressed in this book are strictly my own, and don't necessarily reflect the views and opinions of those affiliated with the garden.

For the most part, these pages convey what I've learned from listening to the garden with a mytho-poetic ear. Does the garden speak? Absolutely! Sometimes it speaks in words, other times not. My hope is that some of what the garden has communicated to me about life, the world, and our place in it will resonate with you, the reader.

## THE FOUNDATIONS OF THE GARDEN

Any garden requires ground work, and Lan Su Chinese Garden was no exception, especially since the site for the garden was originally a parking lot. In a similar way, it would be difficult, if not impossible, to understand the garden without first doing a little digging in order to unearth some of the philosophical and spiritual differences between East and West.

M y first visit to the garden was Valentine's Day, 2003—a perfect day to fall in love with a person or, in my case, a place. I knew from the get-go that Lan Su was like no garden I'd experienced in the West. In Portland there are rose and rhododendron gardens, gardens with fountains and streams, and a lovely Japanese garden in the west hills overlooking the city. But Lan Su was different from all these, and I quickly realized that in order to experience it as it is, to let it speak for itself, I'd have to stop superimposing my cultural beliefs and attitudes upon it.

This was easier said than done. It can take years to recognize, and then step out from behind, the societal lenses we've been conditioned to see through. In the West, our lenses have one dominant characteristic that, in my opinion, has left us with a fractured view of the universe and our place in it. And that characteristic is our attachment to dualism.

I recently led a group of freshmen university students on a garden tour. They were taking a class called *Humanity and Nature*. I was instantly struck at how the course title divided one from the other, as if humanity were separate from the natural world. And in our culture, it is. The West has gone to great lengths over the years attempting to prove to itself just how different from nature we human beings are.

Our use of language reveals this split all the time. We talk about getting back to nature, as if we weren't embedded within it already. A brochure I recently received for a workshop on forgiveness put it this way: "As far as we know, there's no such concept as forgiveness in the animal world, or in nature. It's part of the human condition …." This statement reveals the dominant cultural view that humanity and nature are distinct from one another. In his book, *The Wisdom of Wilderness*, author Gerald May cites "stewardship of the environment" as a trendy term that, no matter how well-intended it may be, still severs us from the natural world by putting us in the one-up position of managers or overseers who must remain forever separate from what we manage. Consequently, we treat the earth as if it were some "thing" other than ourselves.

The worldview that underlies a Chinese garden creates no such split. Within the garden, humanity *and* nature becomes humanity *as* nature.

On yet another school tour a student asked, "So how does a Chinese garden promote healing? How does it alleviate suffering?" I was stunned. I'd been leading tours for ten years by this time and had never had an adult ask me that question, let alone a sixteen-year-old.

My answer? In my experience, the garden heals and alleviates suffering by reawakening us to oneness.

*In this place of quiet retreat*
*where the world does not follow,*
*many old afflictions find healing.*

*– Yao Ho*

Eastern philosophy postulates that the universe operates as a unity, totality, or interdependent whole. This philosophy is monistic rather than dualistic. It recognizes the dualities at work in the universe, but sees all of reality as being grounded in a single basic substance or principle. Lan Su Chinese Garden is a living manifestation of this oneness.

The West, on the other hand, has inherited a Greco-Aristotelian philosophical legacy that divides, categorizes, and erects boundaries, thus blinding us to the cohesive cosmic background in which Chinese sages rooted themselves as a way to stay whole amid the often fragmented foreground created by human thinking. Look, and you'll see the devastating consequences of this fragmentation almost everywhere in our culture. I believe our planet is suffering not from an environmental or climatic illness, but a human illness. And this illness can't be cured scientifically, politically, technologically, or economically because it's a disease of the human spirit, heart, and mind. Separation is the illness. Oneness is the cure.

*Using thinking to try and solve the problems created by thinking*
*is like stirring muddy water in the hope of making it clear.*

*– Laozi*

It's beyond the scope of this book to unravel all the political, social, historical, and philosophical twists and turns that brought us to where we are in the West. (For a concise overview I recommend Darrin Drda's book, *The Four Global Truths: Awakening to the Peril and Promise of Our Times*.) I do feel confident saying, however, that our disconnection and alienation from life stem from our identification with thinking as who and what we are. And the roots of this identification can be traced to the ancient Greek Pre-Socratic philosophers Heraclitus and Parmenides; and later to Socrates, Plato, and Aristotle. In essence, what I hear all of them saying is this:

*You know, the gods and goddesses in our Greek stories are too much like human beings. In fact, they often behave worse than human beings. So let's put the myths through which we've tried to make sense of life and the world on the shelf. From now on, it will be through observation, reason, and logic that we'll come to understand the natural laws of the universe and our place in it. What's more, by skillfully honing the intellect, we'll increase our chance of answering the question: "Is there, indeed, one supreme Reality that underlies the multiplicity of the universe? And, if so, what is it?"*

This shift to seeking truth through reason and logic instead of through myth and metaphor gradually reshaped our consciousness—so much so that, over time, human *thinking* eventually overshadowed human *being*. Perhaps the most cogent example of the culmination of this shift comes from the 17th century French philosopher, René Descartes, who coined the famous statement, "Cogito ergo sum—I think, therefore I am."

Descartes' words put a capstone on the West's identification with thinking alone as a self or "me," an identification set in motion by the Greek Socratic and Pre-Socratic philosophers that gained momentum over the centuries right down to our present day. His statement drove the definitive axe between subject and object, matter and consciousness into the Western psyche. Consequently, we live our lives caught in this illusory split between the me inside our head and what appears to be outside, or not me (the environment and so-called "others," for example).

Named after Descartes himself, Cartesian dualism was, in my opinion, the final nudge that pushed us way over into the left hemisphere of the brain, which prioritizes the rational over the intuitive and the abstract over the concrete. Thus, we live in a society that values virtual over actual, technological rather than organic, and intellectual knowledge over and above a felt connection to the sensory intelligence inherent in our bodies.

*Can you see through your wandering mind*
*and rest in the primordial Oneness?*

*– Laozi*

To take Laozi's question one step further, can you close the mind-made gap between subject and object so completely that there's no longer a you separate from the oneness, but only *the oneness resting as itself*?

So how do you close this illusory gap? Start by looking within. Have you noticed movements going on inside you that continually fluctuate between wanting this and not wanting that? Liking one thing and not liking another? Are you aware of the voice in your head that believes it knows what should or shouldn't be happening in any given situation, and that puts a lot of energy into pulling in what enhances you and pushing away what doesn't?

These conditioned movements of mind comprise what we call the ego. More verb than noun, ego is the dualistic organizing and interpreting of life that goes on inside us all the time. It's the running mental commentary that continually separates this from that, other from self, self from the environment, us from them, divinity from humanity, and so on.

Not surprisingly, the more we identify with these movements within us that break down and divide, the less connected we feel to the whole of life. We suffer a felt lack of oneness, which our ego then tries to fill by pushing us to be more and to get more. It keeps us working very hard, individually and collectively, trying to manipulate and control life in order to convince itself (and other egos) that it's real, right, solid, and safe.

Now multiply all this by over five-hundred million people in North America alone who are, for the most part, unconsciously striving to secure from their fragmenting ego a stable and integrated identity it can't possibly provide. Is it any wonder, then, that most of us spend our lives compulsively seeking ways to get ourselves together? Conditioned to view life through our ego's fracturing lens, is it really all that surprising why so many humans are inflicting so much brokenness and suffering on the planet, other species, and each other?

Please understand, I'm not suggesting we need to get rid of our ego, but that we misuse our ego's movements when we use them to build a self-image separate from everything else. And an image isn't real; it's just a representation. Using your ego to create an image of yourself is like pulling a spoon out of the drawer to chop firewood. A spoon can't function as an axe, and the ego becomes dysfunctional when you try to use it as a self. Recognizing when you're pulling your ego-based self out of the drawer, and knowing when to put it back by dis-identifying from it, are the first steps toward healing yourself, others, and the planet.

I once heard spiritual teacher Adyashanti say that we need just enough ego so as not to put our food into the mouth of the person sitting next to us at the table. I still consider this a good gauge as to whether our relationship to the ego is balanced or imbalanced.

*It isn't about changing how you think.*
*It's about stepping beyond*
*the you who thinks.*

*It isn't a matter of finding your way.*
*It's about losing the you*
*that thinks it's lost.*

*It has nothing to do*
*with improving your life.*
*It's realizing that when*
*you let go of having a life,*
*in favor of being life,*
*everything improves.*

*Nor does it involve having what you want,*
*or wanting what you have.*
*Rather, it's about being free*
*of the you who wants.*

*It isn't a process of finding*
*then stepping through*
*the right spiritual door.*
*It's about opening to the truth*
*that you've never*
*been outside.*

Now let's shift our lens to the 5th century BCE in China. This is the Warring States period, and the country's in tumult. Warlords run rampant, seizing power whenever and wherever they can, and everyone's life hangs by a thread.

Several philosophical schools attempt to bring order to the chaos. One such school, the Confucian, is comprised of the philosopher Kongzi (Confucius) and his followers. Another is a loosely knit group of shamanic-based practitioners and philosophers called Daoists who follow the "Way" (Dao in Chinese means "way" or "path"). Daoists practice a variety of meditation and body cultivation techniques aimed at fostering longevity and attunement with the Dao as it manifests through nature. (I'll discuss some of the philosophical differences between Daoist and Confucian approaches to creating social order later in this chapter.)

From among the Daoists, someone who's come to be known as Laozi (which means "old master") authored a manual (or compiled it from oral sources) on the art of governing and living. This manual is entitled the *Daodejing*, or the *Book of the Virtue of the Way*, and is one of the most translated books in history, second only to the Bible.

This early Daoist philosophy of life expressed in the *Daodejing* became known as *daojia*, which both preceded and differs from Daoist religion, or *daojiao*. Daoist religion began with the charismatic figure Zhang Daoling, who instituted the *Celestial Masters* sect, along with Daoist clergy, in 142 CE.

Labeling the earlier *daojia* tradition a philosophy seems to me to be a misnomer. Certainly, this period did give rise to the classic philosophical teachings of Laozi, Zhuangzi, and Liezi. But, for the most part, *daojia* was an informal way of life that could be followed by anyone, educated noble and illiterate peasant alike. There was no priesthood, no compiled canon, no dogmas or doctrines. The primary teacher was nature, and the human student's assignment, if you will, was to learn through close observation how to live in harmony with its cycles and rhythms.

Like the ancient Greek philosophers, Daoists utilized observation and reason to understand the workings of the universe, but this is where the two part company. For the Daoist, observation and reason can only take us so far. They can provide a finger pointing to the ultimate Reality (Dao), but we can never know that Reality intellectually or conceptually. Why? Because the supreme Reality underlying the universe *is not a form*. It's completely formless, and forms are all our minds can wrap themselves around. Even our thoughts are energetic forms. This is why the first stanza of the *Daodejing* reads: "The Dao that can be named isn't the eternal Dao." This line is a jab at the Confucians who had little or no use for a Dao that couldn't be intellectually grasped, and so remained forever beyond rational human discourse. Dao, for the Confucian, was more a Dao of ethics and morality that, over time, was reduced to little more than a term for an abstract universal principle. Dao for a Daoist, however, was the formless "Dao of heaven," an unseen but living Reality that we can intuit (right brain) and experientially be, but not intellectually know.

*Darkness within darkness, the source of all knowing.*

*– Laozi*

What is darkness within darkness? The mind that knows it doesn't know.

*There was an old farmer who lived with his son. One morning, they awoke to discover all their horses had broken through the fence during the night and were gone. Word quickly got around, and their neighbors gathered to console them. "Oh, what a terrible loss! What bad luck! We're so sorry for your misfortune!" the neighbors moaned. The old farmer looked at them and quietly responded, "We'll see."*

*The next day, the farmer's horses returned, bringing with them a herd of wild horses. The neighbors heard about this, and quickly re-assembled outside the farmer's door. "Oh, what wonderful luck! Now you have three times the number of horses you had before!" The old man simply smiled and said, "We'll see."*

*The following morning, the farmer's son was trying to ride one of the wild horses. The horse threw him, and the son's leg was broken. Within an hour, the neighbors returned. "How awful!" they wailed. "Your son is your main source of support and does most of the farm work. What a tragic thing to have happen!" Once again, the farmer uttered nothing except, "We'll see."*

*The next afternoon, a battalion of soldiers came through the village conscripting all the young men into the army. They passed over the farmer's son, however, because of his broken leg. The neighbors returned and cheered! "What a lucky thing your son broke his leg while trying to break that horse! He might have been conscripted and killed, and then where would you be?" "We'll see," the old man chuckled, "We'll see …."*

*The individual petal cannot see*
*the entire flower.*
*The entire flower cannot see*
*the totality of the field.*

*Why is it that you*
*can look and look*
*and never see*
*the Dao?*

*Because you are*
*looking from it.*

*Step out of knowing*
*into the fragrance*
*that has no walls.*

*A student asked master Yun-men, "What is Dao?"*

*"Walk on!" Yun-men replied.*

Despite all this emphasis on not knowing, I imagine there could still be a mind out there that, like Yun-men's student, is asking, "But what is Dao?"

Alas, to ask, "What is it?" is to have already missed it. Dao isn't a what or an it. Having no beginning or end, Dao is self-blazing (*ziran*), or self-generative. Dao requires nothing outside of Dao in order to be Dao. From this we might conclude that Dao is, but this also misses the mark as Dao is beyond and prior to opposites like is and isn't. Dao simply can't be conceptualized. At best, Dao can be felt as the intelligent, rhythmic, cyclic flow of nature we witness both beyond and within us.

To make Dao more palpable, I occasionally ask a tour group, "So, is there anyone here who's where they thought they'd be at this point in their life?" If most of those present have had ample life experience, I will see heads shaking side to side. And, if someone nods, I'm skeptical.

Even with all our planning, scheming, organizing, and scripting, our lives typically wind up looking not quite (or not at all) like what we thought they would. This is because there's a larger Reality going on that can't be scripted. And it's this larger Reality or Intelligence that continually shapes and patterns our way in the world. The ego calls this "life getting in the way." The Chinese call it "Dao."

*The afternoon knows what the morning never suspected.*

*– Robert Frost*

In the *Daodejing* it's written: "The universe follows Dao, and Dao follows only itself." Simply put, Dao doesn't follow a mechanical, linear, or externally imposed legal order, but its own spontaneous non-legal order (*wuze*). The universe, in turn, follows and reflects Dao's orderly spontaneity or *li*, which I'll discuss later. Not a mechanism or machine made up of independently functioning parts, the cosmos blossoms and proliferates as a relational process whereby everything comes into and passes out of existence interdependently. Daoists referred to this process as mutual arising (*xiangsheng*). The Buddhists had a similar insight, but termed it dependent origination.

Call it what you will, what this points to is that nothing in the universe, including what I call my "self," exists by itself separate from everything else. Sound can be heard because there are ears to hear it. Sunlight exists because there are eyes to see it and forms to feel and reflect it. Plants and humans literally live off one another's breath. When you awaken to this at a deeply felt level, what you begin to realize is that it's taking nothing less than the interaction of the entire cosmos to bring what you call "you" into existence at this very moment. Which raises the question: who and what are you, really? The little you in your head? Or the totality of the universe manifesting as this moment?

*The sun that rises doesn't rise.*
*The sun that sets doesn't set.*

*What appears to our eyes to be two, isn't.*

*Beneath the one sky that is my true skin*
*myriad celestial bodies shine.*

*Where do I begin or end?*

*A Chinese garden is a living example of what can happen
when it isn't assumed that humanity and nature
are separate from and at war with one another.*

*Imagine you're walking beside a lake or stream. Or maybe you're standing on the small, arched granite bridge that crosses over the water directly in front of the garden's waterfall. Looking down, a sunlit whirlpool catches your attention. Notice how the whirlpool isn't part of the water—it is the water. It's a transitory differentiation of the lake that whirls into existence for a time and then unravels and whirls out. But it's always the lake. The whirlpool simultaneously embodies where it's come from, where it is, and where it's heading. It's the lake appearing out of itself, patterning within itself, and disappearing back into itself. Lake. Lake. Lake.*

Like the whirlpool, you and I arise within the generative oneness of the universe and then vanish back into it when our bodies die. Or, to put it another way, we are Dao, birthing, living, and death-ing Dao. Differentiations? Yes. Separation? No.

ONE WITH NATURE

Daoism emphasizes our oneness with nature. It teaches us to move with, rather than against, the ever-changing flow of life and the natural world. A Chinese garden is an embodiment of this philosophy. It's a living example of what can happen when it isn't assumed that humanity and nature are separate from and at war with one another.

Daoism, Confucianism, and Buddhism are referred to as The Three Teachings in China, and all three were at odds with one another at various times in Chinese history. But the opposition between Daoists and Confucians about how to live life well and how to bring order to society had a long history prior to Buddhism's entry into China (around 100 CE). What follows is one example of how these two philosophies differ from each other.

Confucian philosophy (*ru*) aimed at developing four basic virtues: sincerity and benevolence (*ren*); justice, duty, and obligation to others (*yi*); ritual observance (*li*), whereby the Confucian outwardly expressed benevolence and obligation to others; and wisdom (*zhi*). Clearly, these virtues could produce well-cultured and noble men. So where did Daoists and Confucians part company?

Perhaps the simplest way to approach this question is by first looking at what Daoists and Confucians agreed upon, namely the world of non-human nature. Both groups revered nature as the quintessential teacher—although for somewhat different reasons. A Daoist would say mountains and rivers can lead to Dao, whereas a Confucian tended to see mountains and rivers leading to human qualities, such as virtue and moral uprightness. A mountain, for example, could instill in human beings the virtue of steadfastness; a river, the constant flow of benevolence. Here we get a glimpse into one of the key differences between these two groups.

Rather than bringing forth virtue from within himself, the Daoist saw the Confucian placing it outside himself as an object to be emulated or attained. This left the Confucian little choice but to study, analyze, and discuss virtue in order to come up with the best means to acquire it. And as Daoists were quick to point out, this approach ran the risk of the means to an end becoming ends in themselves.

For a Daoist, however, virtue required looking inside yourself and seeing that landscape and humanity were one and the same Dao manifesting as nature. Be this oneness, said the Daoist, and the virtue already inherent within you will rise effortlessly to the surface like a mountain spring. This teaching is akin in Christianity to the words of St. Augustine, "Love, and do what you will."

So on the one hand there was Confucianism, which attempted to mold humanity from the outside through rules and prescribed civic protocols aimed at cultivating social order, virtuousness, and right conduct; and, on the other hand, Daoism, which held that we didn't need to be molded—only redirected to look within and realize Dao is who and what we are. If those in power could do this in their own lives, say the Daoists, they could then help the populace do the same. The imbalance and disharmony created by people chasing after externals and misusing things in an attempt to find themselves would be minimized; balance, harmony, and virtue would flourish; and we'd have the social order we crave.

THE VINEGAR TASTERS

*A Daoist, a Confucian, and a Buddhist were walking down a hot dusty road on a summer's day. They'd been exchanging views for some time and, being thirsty, arrived at the outskirts of a small village where they happened upon what looked like a rain barrel full of water sitting alongside an abandoned hut. Little did they know that the barrel was filled with vinegar. Removing the lid, the Buddhist dipped the ladle in, took a sip, and winced. "Yes, life is bitter suffering!" the Buddhist said to himself. The Confucian was next. He'd seen the Buddhist make a face and so was hesitant to drink, but feeling bound by duty did so anyway. "Ugh! Sour like life!" he sputtered. Finally, it was the Daoist's turn. He raised the ladle to his lips and drank. "Ah! Life is sweet!" the Daoist thought, and a huge smile stretched across his face.*

The moral? What you think is what you drink.

Life tastes different in the garden. It's a place where suffering and bitterness can be transcended and transformed.

Certainly, there are Confucian and Buddhist influences here, but be that as it may the garden has always tasted more Daoist to me. Apparently, I'm not alone in this regard. I recall reading somewhere that the scholar-official who owned a garden during the Ming and Qing dynasties (1368–1911 CE) was "Confucian when he was at work in the world, and Daoist when he was in his garden." This is a revealing glimpse into how the scholar utilized a garden to balance out his life.

## A DAOIST UTOPIA

The Chinese scholar-official wasn't what we think of when we think of a scholar in the West. Chinese scholars were highly educated, but they were essentially bureaucrats employed by the emperor to oversee some aspect of the imperial bureaucracy. And, like many of us today, they liked what the city had to offer, but also wanted a place of quiet and retreat away from their duties and responsibilities.

A garden provided this, and more. It was an oasis of tranquility amid the hustle and bustle of life in an urban center, but it was also a living expression of the scholar's most cherished ideals, beliefs, and philosophical insights. In the words of Educational Institute of Suzhou instructor, Xu Xian, the garden was a "Daoist utopia" within which a scholar devoted himself to intellectual, physical, artistic, and spiritual refinement in the hope he might one day become a Daoist Immortal. An Immortal could be anyone—male or female, rich or poor, educated or uneducated—who had cultivated and transmuted his or her physical and psychical energies to be so in synch with the Dao that the world of opposites, including birth and death, no longer had power over them. They were simply life living itself, or Dao Dao-ing Dao.

In addition to being a civil servant, the Chinese scholar was also what we might call a gentleman of refinement, or a scholar-artist. Think of the scholar as a painter—but instead of paint on his palette he had water, rocks, architecture, poetry, and plants. The scholar used these traditional elements to design and build his garden, but arranged them in a way that revealed his own personal refinement and good taste.

### LAN SU YUAN

The poetic name of Portland's Chinese garden is *Lan Su Yuan* or "Garden of Awakening Orchids," inspired by the garden's *Bletilla striata* terrestrial orchids (*lan*) that bloom in spring and summer. There's a lot of word play in Chinese. As such, *Lan Su Yuan* also means "Portland Suzhou Garden"—Lan coming from PortLANd, and Su from the city of SUzhou, which is located about fifty miles west of Shanghai. For centuries, Suzhou has been *the* city of gardens in China. Lan Su is the centerpiece of a sister-city relationship with Suzhou that began in the mid 1980s. As part of that relationship, Suzhou received a fire truck and a rose garden, and Portland received *Lan Su Yuan*, which opened on 14 September 2000 at a cost of just over twelve-and-a-half million dollars.

### LAND OF FISH AND RICE

It's no coincidence that so many scholars' gardens were built in and around Suzhou. As an affluent center for silk production and luxury goods, Suzhou was a magnet for artists, intellectuals, wealthy merchants, and literati from all over the empire. In the West, we use the term "land of milk and honey" to describe a place of wealth and abundance. From the 14th to the 19th century, Suzhou's prosperity led to it being dubbed "land of fish and rice."

Places of peace and plenty appear, again and again, in Chinese legend and folklore. Long before Suzhou became synonymous with the good life (*xianqing*), the 5th century poet Tao Yuanming penned the following story. He entitled it *Peach Blossom Spring* (*Taohua Yuan*).

Many years ago, an old fisherman headed off into the mountains to find a secluded fishing spot. Happening upon a winding stream, he decided to follow it. Rounding a bend, he was astounded to see the stream flanked on both sides by blossoming peach trees. Wading upstream beneath the canopy of fragrant blooms, he came to the face of a mountain where a spring fed the stream from a small cave. Peering inside, he saw what looked like a glowing light. Intrigued, the old man squatted down, squeezed his thin wiry frame into the narrow cleft and crawled, more than walked, until he came out the other side.

What he saw as he stepped into the broad daylight was so beautiful that it brought tears to his tired, aging eyes. Spread out before him was an idyllic and serene sun-filled valley covered with carefully tended fields and farms. Bountiful crops filled each plot of land, orchards hung heavy with fruit, and ponds rippled with fish. In the distance, he could see simply dressed people working the fields, while others played with children or chatted pleasantly with each other outside of well-tended modest homes. Laughter and the smell of cooking food filled the air. The entire scene spoke peace, abundance, and contentment.

*When the villagers spotted the old man they were terribly surprised and asked where he came from. After he answered all their questions, they invited him to a sumptuous meal. As he ate, village elders described how their forebears discovered this hidden land while fleeing the tumult of the Qin dynasty (221–207 BCE). Removed from the chaos of so-called "civilization," they and their descendants had lived here peacefully ever since. Some elders, however, were curious about events outside, so the fisherman shared what he knew of world affairs, describing great dynasties that rose then fell due to political corruption and rebellion. He painfully recounted wars that had ravaged the land, and how the common people suffered. And as he spoke, those listening shook their heads and sighed in sad amazement.*

*After staying many days, the fisherman took his leave of the people and the place. And as he was departing, a village elder said: "There's no need to tell people on the outside about what you found here."*

*When he arrived home, however, the fisherman couldn't contain his excitement. He told the local prefect about the hidden land and where he'd found it. Word got around, and soon many of the townspeople were trying to retrace the route based on what the old fisherman had said. But no matter how hard they looked they never found the stream or the peach trees. And when they arrived at where the cleft in the mountain face should have been, there wasn't so much as a crack.*

A PLACE OF THE HEART

Luckily for us, *Peach Blossom Spring* is no longer just a story. Nor is it a place that can be lost—here one moment, gone the next. A place of the heart, *Peach Blossom Spring* is Lan Su Yuan. It's the Beyond within.

# The Beyond Within

Isn't this our work?
To let ourselves be drawn so deeply into the Earth
that what appears to lie beyond
reawakens within us as ourselves.

– Rilke

I stand facing east, where all things begin. I stand here, not there. Not where I should be, or want to be, or could be. Not where I was yesterday or where I may or may not be tomorrow, but here, now. I stand before the garden's main gate, this narrow portal that reminds me of the cleft in the mountain face from the story *Peach Blossom Spring*, as if I were standing in front of one of those Metro transit maps in Paris with an arrow pointing to the red dot that says: *vous êtes ici … you are here.* Like most of us, I sadly spend most of my time racing to get from here to there when my real spiritual task is getting from there to here. So I take time before entering the garden to check in with myself and ask, "Am I really here?"

As a child, I recall riding a ferry on Kootenay Lake in British Columbia, Canada. We were heading from Balfour to Crawford Bay, about a thirty-minute trip. Fifteen minutes into our journey, the ferry heading the other direction appeared to one side of us. I remember getting quite upset because the other ferry seemed to be moving incredibly fast, and we were moving so slowly!

On the way home we switched ferries. I was thrilled because now we were on the fast ferry I'd seen just a couple hours before. Sure enough, within fifteen minutes the ferry we'd first taken appeared off to one side—except now it was moving fast and we were moving slowly!

My ferry ride is a metaphor for how most of us see and live our lives. Life frequently appears to be moving the way we want it to everywhere except where we are. And so we live life constantly on the run, trying to get from here to there. Like my ferry experience, however, when *there* becomes *here* it can lose its mystique and allure because where we are often fails to live up to our projected fantasies about where we're not. This can leave us scanning the future horizon from the bow of our days hoping we'll glimpse life coming toward us from somewhere other than where we are. Or, standing aft, we fixate on the past, searching life's wake for clues as to where we went wrong.

Have you noticed that life is always precisely as it is, regardless of what your mind thinks about it? Have you stopped long enough to realize that you're always exactly where you are no matter how persistently your thinking pulls you from here to there?

*I've stopped. You haven't.*

*– Buddha.*

## BETWEEN TWO WORLDS

The garden's entry plaza is a transitional space. Here I stand between two worlds, but already the noisy city streets and high-rise buildings have begun to fade to the periphery. With every step, I'm moving beyond the everyday human world into another reality.

Along the plaza's north wall are a plum tree, a pine, and a stand of bamboo. In China these are called the Three Friends of Winter (*suihan sanyou*) because all three thrive during the coldest season. Together, they symbolize endurance and perseverance. And although winter may still be months away, they remind me how relationships sustain us through all sorts of harsh weather.

Set amid the Three Friends is a ten-foot tall, crescent-shaped ashen stone. Narrow at the bottom, heavy at the top, it seems to float in mid-air like a wisp of swirling fog. Without uttering a single word it says:

*Let go. Here's where all your heaviness becomes light.*

*Have you noticed that life is always precisely as it is,
regardless of what your mind thinks about it?*

S tepping through the garden's main gate, I enter the Tranquility Courtyard. Within seconds I feel my body slow down as I transition from outer to inner space. The courtyard's white walls, plants, shaded stone-patterned floor, and adjoining covered walkway embrace me, drawing my attention to the tranquility that lies both within the garden and within myself. Like most of us, I spend much of my life focused on externals. My mind constantly contracts around people, places, and objects, generating opinions, ideas, judgments, regrets, desires, and so on that pull me out of myself and out of the present moment. Inside the garden these contractions subside, reawakening me to my innermost self, or what the 19th century poet Gerard Manley Hopkins called "inscape."

Like the garden, inscape requires nurturing, cultivation, and attention. It demands that I continually cut back the overgrowth of noise in my head so the flower of the present moment remains visible.

Visible, yes, but the present moment is also that which is invisible. As spiritual teacher and author Eckhart Tolle reminds us in one of his talks, the present moment is not only *what takes place*, but the empty silent space *within which everything takes place*. Tolle goes on to point out that this moment is all we really have. Take time now to consider this for yourself:

> *When you began reading this book, you did so in the present moment. When you finish in the so-called future, you'll do so in the present moment. Reading these words, you're reading them in the present moment. This moment is all there is. And the quickest way to step out of what is, is by thinking yourself into what was or might be.*

Staying open to life in the moment promotes tranquility and sanity. And, for me, nothing in the garden conveys what it means to remain open to "what is" more eloquently than the Four-Sided Hall.

FOUR-SIDED HALL

On the north side of the Tranquility Courtyard stands the beautiful Four-Sided Hall (*tingtang*). Like all buildings and pavilions in the garden, this hall has a pitched blue-gray tiled roof that sweeps up gracefully at each corner. This gives the structure an almost otherworldly feel, as if it were ascending into the heavens like a mountain peak or scaly dragon. Here, beneath the hall's steeply sloping roof, the scholar-official received and entertained guests—especially important guests like royalty, dignitaries, fellow scholars, and high officials.

This building also has two poetic names: the Lotus Hall, named after the lotus flowers that bloom in the lake on the north side of the hall's terrace during summer; and Hall of Brocade Clouds, inspired by wispy reflections of clouds lacing in and out of one another like silky brocade on the water's surface. The generic term "Four-Sided Hall" refers to the four walls that really aren't walls at all. They're floor-to-ceiling windows set into lavishly carved tracery frames. From the inside, these frames turn the garden into a kaleidoscope of natural vistas. The see-through walls also let the inside out and the outside in, thus blurring our illusory distinctions between what's inner and what's outer; or, for that matter, what's human and what's nature.

*My window frames ancient mountains—*
*cloudy crags and jagged scarps towering above deep ravines.*

*Truly, just living with a view of peaks like this*
*can change a person's heart forever.*
*What need then to go searching for my walking stick?*
*my battered trekking shoes?*
*Only people lost in the fog of separation*
*see things as close or far.*

Like most of us in the West, I've been conditioned to believe that I'm me walking around inside this sack of skin and everything outside me isn't me. But is that true? Are the fish in the water, or is the water also in the fish? Am I in the environment, or is the environment also in me? When my body dies, it will become the temperature of whatever the surrounding environment is. In the garden, what I come to realize, again and again, is what Daoist and Buddhist sages have always known—that on the level of form *I am the environment* seeing, hearing, smelling, touching, and tasting itself.

*Can you live as the world rather than in the world?*
*Can you awaken each morning as the day, rather than to it?*
*Can you let yourself become what you see,*
*rather than turning what you see into yourself?*

When a Chinese scholar-official passed the imperial exams to work for the government (which provided the money needed to build and maintain something as costly as a garden) he was congratulated by his peers for "plucking the blossom from the Moon Palace." In China, the osmanthus bush or tree (*gui*) *is* the Moon Palace because its small and sweet-smelling white flowers bloom during the Moon Festival in late October. Having passed his exams in Beijing, the scholar took a sprig of osmanthus from the capital back to his home town where he planted it as a symbol of his achievement.

Using the osmanthus as his mentor, a scholar strove to remain rooted in noble uprightness amid recurring storms of political corruption and intrigues within the imperial court. Like the tree's scented flowers, I imagine him being called upon, again and again, to live his life of public service openly and authentically, holding none of his fragrance back. By attuning his senses to something as tiny as an osmanthus blossom, the scholar put into practice the Confucian teaching that only by keeping our eyes open to small things can we hope to perceive life's larger design.

*When the root is deep, there's no need to fear the wind.*

*– Chinese proverb*

*The scent of one blossoming osmanthus tree*
*fills the entire neighborhood.*

*The aroma from a single one of its flowers*
*wafts through every room.*

*Those who notice the fragrance, notice.*
*Those who don't, don't.*

*Readiness is everything.*
*Without it, who can recognize*
*that sweet perfume permeating*
*within and without?*

*Serene, silent,*
*the tree wants nothing,*
*asks nothing.*

*Ignore it, curse it, praise it,*
*the scent remains untouched.*

*Be like that—*
*your fragrance drifting every direction*
*without discriminating,*
*never withholding life from life.*

*I am the environment ... seeing, hearing, smelling,*
*touching, and tasting itself.*

Our garden isn't really one garden—it's a collection of compartmentalized gardens set within the larger square framework of four outer walls. It's a microcosm of the universe in that it manifests in multiplicity while operating as a oneness or totality.

The garden is a jewel box in the city. Within it, an endless array of sounds, sights, and smells are created by the five key elements that, together, reflect and play off one another like many-faceted gems. Inside, I sometimes wonder, "Am I reaching in and pulling gems out of the garden, or is it reaching in and pulling gems out of me?"

## ENTERING THE WONDERLAND

Flowers and blossoms are the quintessential jewels in the garden, and many have symbolic value. A guest visiting a garden hundreds of years ago would have known what various trees, flowers, and plants signified and why they were planted where they were planted.

Flora and fauna are also depicted artistically in the garden. For example, set in stone into the Tranquility Courtyard floor is a recurring stylized crab-apple blossom pattern that visually leads us to a crab-apple blossom portal in the east wall. In China, crab-apple blossoms symbolize springtime and new life. There's also a play on words in Chinese between the word for crab apple, *haitang* and *tang* or "hall," the central dwelling of an ancient Chinese home. Thus, our blossom-shaped entry could be seen as a doorway through which we come home to our true selves and to our oneness with nature. It's a threshold where, with a single step, we can blossom into new ways of relating to life, others, and ourselves. As the inscription over this petaled portal reminds us, we are "Entering the Wonderland." We're crossing over into another world.

*The garden is a jewel box in the city.*

M y partner and I recently ate dinner at a trendy new neighborhood restaurant. The place had been busy every night since it opened and reservations were hard to get. When we sat down at our table there were very few people inside but, within about twenty minutes, the space went from nearly empty to full, and practically silent to noisy. Shortly after, rock music came on through overhead speakers. Not surprisingly, patrons' voices escalated in order to be heard. I asked our waitress if the music might be turned down. She said she'd check on it. I looked around at the other tables. None of the other customers appeared to be impacted or irritated by this dinnertime din, but by the time we left we both had headaches.

We live in a human world that, in my experience, has become increasingly frenetic and abrasive. Restaurant scenarios like mine aren't uncommon. People seem desensitized to noise and distraction. Many, it seems, actually crave it.

Could our frenzy, noise, and accelerating pace be linked to our waning ability to experience wonder? Is our pandemic addiction to so-called "connection" technology due to our disconnection from the wonder of life? Do we keep increasing sensory stimulation in order to feel alive? Having lost our sense of wonder, are we looking in all the wrong places for replacements that give us a momentary jolt, but never really satisfy? The short-lived novelty of a bigger-and-better shopping mall, for instance, or louder and louder movies that max out decibel levels in an attempt to break through our numbness and induce us with an "experience." Throughout our culture, almost everything is touted as an experience—your shopping experience. Your banking experience. Your driving, customer service, hair-styling, credit card, TV experience.

Sadly, all of these are nothing more than shallow substitutes for the deep experience of aliveness that comes with wonder. They're indicative of a culture that, having lost touch with wonder, settles instead for the adrenaline rush or "hit" that inevitably leads to our "Been there, done that. What's the next thing?" attitude toward life.

*Too many colors blind the eye.*
*A constant barrage of sound deafens the ear.*
*Plate after plate of flavors deadens the taste.*
*An endless stream of thoughts weakens the mind.*
*Countless desires shrivel up the heart.*

*– Laozi*

So if our sense of aliveness depends on our ability to sustain wonder, what's our sense of wonder contingent on? What I'd like to suggest is that wonder spontaneously arises when we slow down long enough to feel and be life, instead of just thinking about and commenting on it, which both create distance. Wonder reappears when we remove the conceptual cataracts from our eyes that can blind us to lived experience.

## WHAT'S ACTUALLY HERE

Imagine your thoughts are like an invasive Himalayan blackberry bush that, once it roots in your yard, takes over everything. Notice how your thought-brambles insinuate themselves between you and what's taking place. This might involve a place, another person, or a situation. Be aware of how you separate yourself from the moment by identifying with the mental commentary in your head. When this occurs, you'll probably notice you react on a felt level to what you're telling yourself, but you've separated yourself from what's actually here.

*Recall seeing a sunset. As soon as you move into a mental commentary about or evaluation of it such as, "Oh! Isn't it beautiful!" you've conceptualized the moment by turning it into a thought. You've reduced the felt living reality to a mere abstraction.*

Wonder isn't a concept. It's a felt experience of awe or marvel. And in order to remain open and receptive to wonder, we have to stay rooted in the moment. We need to remember *it's beauty itself* that causes wonder, not our thoughts *about it*.

*Beauty begets wonder. And life is to be lived in wonder.*

*– Father Paschal Cheline, OSB*

Another way we lose touch with wonder is when we take life and beauty for granted. What's important is that we stay awake to the miracle that something is happening rather than nothing.

The 17th century English physician and author Thomas Browne said we carry inside us the wonder we seek outside. If this is true (and I believe it is), then the garden inscription "Entering the Wonderland" is really a finger pointing back at me. It's a reminder that stepping into the garden is, in essence, stepping into the wonder of my deepest and truest self. It's where I enter the Beyond within.

STRINGS OF PEARLS

Nothing within the garden is as it seems. Things morph into other things before our eyes, blurring that thin line between dream and what we call reality. Hard stones set into courtyard floors become soft crab-apple blossoms and lake-water designs. Flowers and trees become poems, and poems become the visitors who read them. Planted beside the Painted Boat in Misty Rain Pavilion, a windblown willow (*chuiliu*) billows like a sail, while beads of rain dripping from the bluish gray bat-shaped drip tiles that run all along the garden's roofline glisten like strings of pearls. And, to a poetic eye, might the covered bridge's two curved balustrades even be a double rainbow?

Interestingly, the paradoxes and seeming contradictions in the garden are what give it life and vibrancy. They make it a place of wonder. Here, trees, water, and stones both are and aren't forests, rivers, and mountains. Walls made up entirely of windows both are and aren't walls. Similarly, the garden both is and isn't a landscape painting I not only look at, but enter into and become.

Our garden is a gateway. Metaphor is the key. When I allow myself to experience plants, water, and rocks as the garden's flesh, blood, and bones, this key turns, the gate opens, and I enter the wonderland. Once inside, I can no longer treat what surrounds me as a mere collection of objects foreign to myself. I reawaken to my deep affinity with a living landscape and with the one heart beating at the center of our world. I undergo a transformation from personal to universal.

THE TRANSFORMATION OF THINGS

*The Daoist philosopher Zhuangzi dreamt he was a butterfly fluttering through a field of flowers. Light, carefree, the winged creature flitted petal to petal and leaf to leaf, completely unaware of a Zhuangzi. But when he woke up, there he was, Zhuangzi again for sure! Or was he sure? Was it Zhuangzi who dreamt he was a butterfly, or a butterfly now asleep and dreaming he was Zhuangzi? Certainly there must be a difference between the two! This is what sages call the Great Transformation of Things (taihua).*

Our garden is more than a place of transformation—it is transformation happening, right before our eyes. And perhaps no other element in our garden embodies this continuous process of change more perfectly and profoundly than water.

*The garden both is and isn't a landscape painting*
*I not only look at, but enter into and become.*

# Water/*shui*
# Daoist Principle: *wu wei*

*The Beyond within me is like a silent lakebed.*
*Not the lake, but not separate from it, the lakebed*
*holds the lake and shapes it.*

*– Daniel Skach-Mills*

L ife flows into and out of form, then flows into and out of yet another form, and on and on ad infinitum. This is the endless, fluid play of the formless, nameless Dao. Little wonder then why Daoists hold water in such high regard. Like the Dao, water is flexible, fluid, and nourishes everything indiscriminately without even trying. So flexible, in fact, that it takes the shape of whatever you pour it into. Soft and yielding to be sure, but as it's written in the *Daodejing*:

> *Nothing is as soft and flexible as water.*
> *Yet, for wearing away the rigid and hard,*
> *what can surpass it?*
>
> *– Laozi*

Like the Dao, water is more verb than noun. It's a happening that, at this moment, is simultaneously moving through the atmosphere and flowing as a river. It's a shape-shifter, transforming in perfect accordance with its environment: water, ice, vapor—each is still essentially water. Water, human, animal, plant, universe—each is still essentially Dao.

> *Can you remain flexible like water,*
> *taking the shape of whatever life pours you into?*
> *Can you be like the still lake*
> *that reflects the whole universe while maintaining*
> *its own intrinsic clarity?*

On the eastern side of the garden's crab-apple blossom portal, a gray herringbone tile pathway leads left to the Double Rainbow Covered Bridge, and right to the Knowing the Fish Pavilion. Open on all four sides, this square pavilion (*ting*) serves as a rest stop, a place to linger, look, and listen. Here, overlooking the water, I begin to see through my thinking all the way to the bottom of myself. Like the fish, I can swim beneath whatever's happening on the surface until I reach the still depths within.

More often than I care to admit, my rigid attitudes and thoughts about life muddy my ability to experience what's right in front of me. The following story, entitled "Knowing the Fish," points to this human malady.

*Two philosophers, Zhuangzi and Huizi, were walking along a river. Zhuangzi spied a school of fish and said, "I experience the fish as being really happy today, don't you?" Huizi quickly retorted, "How do you know whether or not the fish are happy? You're not a fish!" Completely unruffled, Zhuangzi replied, "How do you know that I don't know whether or not the fish are happy? You're not me!"*

Can you see in the story how Zhuangzi is the Daoist? He's completely one with nature. Huizi, on the other hand, is more like a Confucian. He's strongly aligned with his thinking and his intellect. And so, when Zhuangzi says to Huizi, "You're not me!" what I hear him saying is this:

*"Huizi, Huizi! You experience life very differently from me! And that's because you're caught in a trance of ideas about life and the world that separates you from experiencing life and the world as yourself. Unlike you, I no longer live constantly in my head. As such, I feel no separation from life, and so can say that I experience the fishes' happiness as my own."*

The key here is oneness. Zhuangzi's joy and the fishes' joy are one and the same joy. And this joy is derived, not from thought, but from a felt oneness with life. Embodying this oneness is essential to experiencing life as what Daoists call an "effortless flow." And this brings us to our first Daoist principle, *wu wei*.

*Wu wei* is often translated "not doing." I like Asia scholar Alan Watts' translation "not forcing" better—not forcing things to happen or not happen. *Wu wei* is about developing our ability to respond to life situations with minimal interference and expenditure of energy.

Contrary to Western misconceptions, *wu wei* isn't about mindlessly walking through life, but it is about bringing less mind and more intuitive awareness to life situations as they arise. This translates into skillfully navigating life rather than fighting against it. It means letting go of the struggle to push or pull the river in the direction our ego thinks it should go.

Nor does *wu wei* advocate an avoidance of conflict. Conflict in life is inevitable. The key is knowing how and when to engage conflict so we don't go against the nature of things or feed the fire. Most of us have been conditioned to fight fire with fire. We've been given one tool to put into our toolbox: a hammer. And, as the old saying goes, "If your only tool is a hammer, everything has to be a nail." A *wu wei* practitioner would be reluctant to fight fire with fire. Extinguishing fire with water is more effective.

> *Pick up a hammer to use it.*
> *Put it down when you're through.*
>
> *Use your own mind like that,*
> *as a tool rather than a self,*
> *and you'll no longer be wielding*
> *what nails you to building yourself up*
> *or knocking others down.*
>
> *You won't even have to lay*
> *a foundation for peace.*

Another misunderstanding is that *wu wei* is about passively going with the flow. If you've ever white-water rafted you know this doesn't work. Certainly there will be placid stretches where you can lay back, relax, and let the river carry you. But if you think the whole journey's going to be like that you're in for a surprise. Eventually you'll hit some rapids, and if you don't know how to navigate them skillfully you could wind up capsizing, or worse.

A *wu wei* master might say that to deftly navigate the current you have to become the current. This is because, when you're dealing with white water or the ever-changing flow of life, there's often little or no time to think about what your next move is going to be. The child walking beside you bolts into a busy street. Do you stop to think, What should I do? Is this the right move? What are all the ramifications? No. Your body's intelligence takes over and you move in response to the moment.

In athletics, this is called being in the zone. Our thinking mind moves out of the way and the game effortlessly plays the game, or the dance dances the dance, or the poem writes the poem. And then, when the game or the dance or the poem is complete, our mind jumps back into the driver's seat and says, "Okay, I'll take over from here, thank you very much!" And so we fail to realize that we can live our entire lives in that zone of effortless oneness in response to what's happening. We can be life responding to itself, picking up thought when we need it and putting it down when we don't.

*O Body swayed to music,*
*O brightening glance*
*How can we know the dancer*
*from the dance?*

*– William Butler Yeats*

*The philosopher Kongzi was walking through a gorge where an enormous waterfall plunged into a turbulent pool. Looking up, he spied an elderly man who appeared to totter and then tumble over the falls. Terrified, Kongzi raced to the edge of the raging water, expecting to save the clumsy fool from drowning. To his surprise, however, the white-haired gent was completely unharmed and strolling happily along the bank!*

*Unable to believe his eyes, Kongzi approached the man and said to him, "Sir, at first I thought you must be some kind of supernatural being, but now I see you're an ordinary man like me. You must tell me, by what means did you manage to survive your plunge over the falls?"*

*The man smiled. "That? Oh, that was nothing," he chuckled. "I simply jumped into the torrent at its center and flowed with the current without imposing my will on it. Then, I exited when the water swirled the other way. This all comes quite naturally to me."*

*"What do you mean by natural?" Kongzi asked.*

*"Well," replied the old man, grinning ear to ear, "you and I both grew up with soil under our feet, and so feel completely at home on land. I was also raised near the river, and so feel perfectly at home in water. Were I to think about how I do these things, it wouldn't flow naturally. Instead, I simply move as the water moves and no harm befalls me."*

What follows is an example of *wu wei* from my own life.

In 1997, I completed a Master's degree in Counseling Psychology. It was a lot of work, and I don't regret having put my time and energy into it. After graduation, I went to work as a psychotherapist for an agency that had been in business twenty years. Two years later, the agency ran into financial problems and dissolved. I went to work for another mental health center which eventually ran into similar difficulties and closed. I opened a private practice and worked with a number of clients over the years. Still, my practice never really blossomed despite all the workshops and classes I facilitated to promote it.

In 2004 I had to back up and take a hard look at what I was doing. Very little where my career was concerned had really panned out. I'd helped some people, but things just didn't seem to be coming together. When the clients I was seeing had all finished their work I decided not to take on anyone new. I closed my practice, not knowing what my next step in life would be.

At some point life and what I was doing had parted company. The wind had changed course and I hadn't adjusted my sail. I could have continued to expend useless effort hammering away at life, trying to force it to go in the direction I wanted my career path to go. Instead, I was able to pause, step back, and open myself to where life was actually heading—although I had no idea where that was.

Shortly after, life began to take on an almost effortless quality. I began teaching, which I enjoyed. I started writing again and, within a few years, a publisher who saw some of my work in print contacted me to see if I had any manuscripts. This led to my first publication, *The Tao of Now*, which virtually wrote itself in about three months. Other books followed, all of which have received some kind of recognition or award. Also around this time, I trained to be a docent for Lan Su Chinese Garden, where I've loved giving tours since 2005.

This experience of life effortlessly coming together has an almost magical quality about it. I think you really have to experience this to know what it's like. "Windows just opened up" is how some people describe it. For me, serendipitous connections occurred that I never could have orchestrated in a hundred years. Some call this synchronicity. True, I had to prepare and teach the classes, write the books, and so forth—but the doing simply flowed. I wasn't doing it. Life seemed to be living or doing itself.

Was my career a failure? In the eyes of the human world, perhaps. But the even greater failure would have been to keep veering farther and farther away from where life was going. As Laozi asks in the *Daodejing*: "Failure? Success? Which is more dangerous?"

*What's the difference between you and a Daoist master?*
*The master expects only what happens.*

### THE MORE YOU RELAX INTO IT, THE FREER YOU BECOME

Have you ever put the tips of your left and right forefingers into one of those tubular Chinese finger traps? If so, you know the more you try to pull your way out by force, the more trapped you become. The more you relax into what's gripping you, the freer you become. That's *wu wei*.

# Architecture/*jianzhu*
# Daoist Principle: *li*

*Though my dwelling stands in the human world*
*I hear no clamor from cart or horse.*
*"How can this be?" you ask.*
*When thinking is distanced,*
*the abode becomes remote.*

*– Tao Yuanming*

*We build walls for a house,*

*but it's the empty spaces in the walls that let in the light.*

*– Laozi*

LOUNGE HALL

T ucked into a shady cove in the garden's southeast corner, the Lounge Hall (*xuan*) is a waterside building (*shuixie*) that is also called the Reflections in Clear Ripples Hall. This poetic name was inspired by the beautiful rippling reflections cast onto the front of the building from sunlight glinting off the water, and by garden scenery reflected in the lake.

Pausing on the walkway in front of the hall, a visitor might catch a breeze on a warm summer day; be dazzled in autumn by crimson leaves of the lace maple (*feng*) shimmering with rain; catch sight of yellow forsythia (*jinzhonghua*) cascading over the lake banks in winter; and, in early spring, be enraptured by the sweet scent of daphne (*ruixiang*) wafting from the east end of the Double Rainbow Covered Bridge.

Inside the Lounge Hall, a scholar-official and his extended family might have spent time telling stories, playing musical instruments, or playing games like *xiangqi* (Chinese chess) or *weiqi* (called *go* in Japan). I like to imagine the interior of this building as the inside living room space, while the rest of the garden is the outside living room space. The flow between the two is facilitated by covered walkways (*langzi*) that function very much like hallways inside a house.

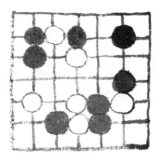

Temples and monasteries, with their peaceful courtyards, serene gardens, and limpid ponds were major influences on Chinese garden architecture and design. They were tranquil spaces designed for meditation and quiet introspection or contemplation.

Little wonder, then, that the generic term for building in Chinese, *guan*—which, according to China scholar Ken Cohen literally means "observatory"—is also the word used for a Daoist or Buddhist monastery, or a Daoist, Buddhist, or Confucian temple.

I like to think of buildings in the garden in this way—as observatories, from which we can quietly contemplate the workings of nature, and within which we can observe our own inner workings. Peering outside, we become as rooted as the tree, as silent as the stone. Looking within, we begin to see beyond our movements of mind that continually pull us out of the present moment, and out of the serenity that the world of non-human nature enjoys most all the time.

*What you think isn't the problem.*
*Believing what you think is the problem.*

Gazing out at the lake through a window in the Lounge Hall, I'm reminded of the Chinese poet Zhang Qian who wrote, "There's nothing like the reflections on lake water to still people's minds."

Zhang Qian was a keen observer and student of nature. Like all Daoists, he revered nature as our quintessential teacher. Clearly, what he learned was that the lake and the world of non-human nature reflected in it—trees, clouds, plants, birds—doesn't stimulate a lot of thinking. It has a calming effect on the human mind. The still lake taught Zhang Qian how to reflect life as it is, not as he thought it should or shouldn't be.

*Remember a time when you were near a pond or lake. Can you recall seeing reflections on the water's surface? The water didn't stir itself up with questions like: Will I reflect it wrong? What does this reflection mean? Will others dislike what I'm reflecting? Should I decide whether or not I like this image before I reflect it? No, the water just is. Can you demonstrate the same mirror-like quality in your own life?*

Another way the garden gets us to notice what nature has to teach is by drawing our attention to it through the use of borrowed or framed views. This is particularly evident inside the buildings where picture windows have been turned into window pictures by framing each space with ornate wooden traceries that highlight the gardenscape beyond. This, in turn, creates a landscape painting effect that draws our attention to the natural vista. Landscape painting also brings us to another Daoist principle, the principle of *li*.

In Chinese, *li* (pronounced "lee," and not to be confused with the *li* in Confucian *ru* philosophy) is the character that refers to the markings in jade. *Li* is the organizing principle underlying the complex array of organic, unrepeatable, and spontaneously occurring patterns we see everywhere in nature: snowflakes, wood grain, ripples in water, the lines in the palm of your hand are all displays of *li*. This fresh and ever-changing aliveness in nature is what Chinese painters are trying to capture when they create a brush painting.

Now we all know how difficult it can be to be spontaneous, especially as we get older. I'd venture to say, from first grade onward, most of our childlike spontaneity is being systematically conditioned out of us. And what replaces it is our critical, judgmental thinking mind that gets in the way of our every move—Will I do it wrong? Will I look stupid? What will others think?

Consider this: have you ever seen a mistake in an ocean wave? Imagine stepping into an old-growth forest and saying, "You know, I think that tree should be moved a little to the left." It sounds ludicrous, but this is what we do to ourselves, others, and the planet all the time.

A number of years ago, I went to a photography exhibit at the Oregon Historical Society. The exhibition focused on the changing face of the Columbia River Gorge over perhaps the past one-hundred fifty years. One black-and-white photo still stands out for me. It was a panoramic shot, taken from one of the high hills overlooking the city of The Dalles in perhaps the 1930s or 40s. What struck me was how the town's blocky, right-angled grid of streets stood out in such stark contrast to the surrounding river-and-hills landscape that was rolling and flowing in every direction.

*Deriving understanding from being who you are is what we call nature.*
*Deriving who you are from understanding is called culture.*

*– Kongzi*

Clearly, there's room for human cultural patterns in the world. In Chinese, the word for culture is *wen*—or, more specifically, human culture is *ren wen*. There are many examples of culture and nature interacting harmoniously within the garden—pavilions reflected in lake water, poetry carved in stone, tea poured into teaware all reflect this well-balanced interaction.

What causes harm is when human culture is out of balance with non-human nature. And this imbalance occurs when we humans lose touch with the larger picture and begin superimposing our cultural patterns onto life as if everything in the world worked according to our linear, gridlocked ways of thinking.

*Harmful spirits travel only in straight lines.*

*– a Chinese saying*

Actually, I find our distinctions between the patterns of human culture and those of nature to be both contrived and illusory. When you get right down to it, since everything is one, then every human-made pattern, from a garden to a toxic garbage dump, is no less a manifestation of *li* in nature than is a beaver dam or bird nest. Still, we seem to have an innate sense that some human patterns are more in harmony with those of non-human nature than others. And the presence or absence of this harmony seems to depend upon whether the human consciousness producing those patterns has awakened to oneness, or is still sleeping the unconscious sleep of separation.

*The world and its ten-thousand things*
*are inside me.*

*– Mengzi*

What I've come to realize over the years is that the garden is really a blend of Daoism, Confucianism, and Buddhism; symmetry and asymmetry; dream and reality; culture and nature all working together to create a balanced and harmonious whole. Little wonder, then, that the more time I spend in the garden the more balanced I seem to be. And the more balanced I am, the greater the likelihood that my behavior will be a harmonious and spontaneous expression of *li* in the world.

*Make the two one.*
*Make what's inner outer*
*and what's outer inner.*
*Then shall you enter the kingdom.*

*– Jesus/Gnostic Gospels*

L eaving the Lounge Hall, we head north beneath one of the garden's many covered walkways toward the Listening to the Fragrance Courtyard. "Listening to the Fragrance" strikes most of us as a rather unusual name. Not so in a Chinese garden, however, where a keen poetic sensibility can bring about a momentary exchange or fusion of the senses called synesthesia. A common phenomenon in Daoism, and in some schools of Buddhism, synesthesia could take a variety of forms. Catching a whiff of wild mint and hearing a "shaken bell tingling the air" is one example. Tasting something spicy hot and "seeing red" is another.

As this courtyard's name suggests, a variety of fragrant species are planted here. Wintersweet (*lamei*) in the northeast corner blooms in late January through early February, while star jasmine (*luoshi*) planted below it is very fragrant in summer. Winter honeysuckle (*jinyinhua*) tucked into the northwest corner produces white scented flowers during the season after which it's named. And on the same side to the south, a waxy leafed *pittosporum*, commonly called mock orange (*haitong*) fills the air with a thick sweet aroma when it blossoms in late spring.

But keep your eyes open. There's also another stone floral design set, or planted if you will, into the courtyard floor. Created almost entirely out of smooth black-and-white rocks, the pattern reminds me of a bed of blooming lotus flowers.

Look again, and you'll notice that practically every stone in this floor is set on edge. This is for a reason. Positioning the stones in this way creates a reflexology foot massage that stimulates a key acupoint on the bottom of your foot. In Chinese medicine, this acupoint is called the *yongquan* or "bubbling spring." Traditional Chinese medicine posits that when bodily energy becomes blocked or stagnant, illness occurs. Walking barefoot across these stones opens the body's energy channels or meridians, which allows our life force or *qi* (pronounced "chee") to flow freely, thus facilitating good health.

## LIVING INK-BRUSH PAINTINGS

This courtyard's reflexology floor gives us occasion to slow down and notice what's right under our feet. Likewise, its blank white walls, surrounding us like unrolled sheets of rice paper, awaken us to what's right before our eyes. Here, nature is the artist. A brushstroke of wind, a splash of sunlight casting shadows through branches and leaves, and voilá! The walls are transformed into a gallery of living ink-brush paintings.

*What's changeless sees what changes.*
*What's still sees what moves.*

*Can you synthesize your senses into one sense,*
*the way rain becomes a stream,*
*and a stream becomes a river,*
*and a river an ocean*
*that takes everything in?*
*Can you feel your body's*
*subtle presence so completely*
*that this, rather than thinking,*
*becomes the source of all your action,*
*the ground of your identity?*

*Tasting a sound,*
*listening to a fragrance.*
*Don't think about it!*
*Do it!*

*Like sunlight soundlessly*
*touching a shiny brass bell,*
*every eye in the room*
*that's struck by it*
*rings.*

In times past, Chinese landscape paintings were painted on scrolls and you'd unroll the scroll a little at a time as if you were traveling through the painting. Similarly, the garden is a three-dimensional scroll painting designed to reveal itself bit by bit. Notice the way walls block your view and how water disappears into infinity under buildings. These design features create a sense of mystery and anticipation. They also make the garden feel larger than it actually is.

Set into the Listening to the Fragrance Courtyard's north wall is a round, open doorway called a moon gate, so named because it symbolizes the full moon. Over the gate are two Chinese characters molded onto a tile plaque. This plaque looks like a partially unrolled scroll, and the inscription on it invites us to "read the landscape" (*du hua*).

What does it mean to read the landscape? To me, it's a reminder that the garden is best "read" with a poetic, rather than a literal eye. Deeper levels of meaning emerge when I approach the garden like a Daoist poem, which would be about natural settings such as mountains, rivers, forests, and lakes.

Poetry has rhythm, and reading the garden poetically is how I experience the rhythm of the place. Feeling this rhythm in my body brings what lies beyond to life within me. It turns the garden's courtyards, buildings, and scenery into a series of living stanzas in a three-dimensional poem that's never twice the same.

In addition to the moon, circles in China can also represent heaven, while squares symbolize earth. I see our round moon gate set into a wall of the square courtyard as a Daoist reminder that heaven and earth are one. All we need are the eyes to see it, and the hearts to feel it.

## THE SCHOLAR'S COURTYARD

Heading north through the moon gate, we enter the Scholar's Courtyard. Similar to the garden's entry plaza, this courtyard is where I check in with myself before reaching the Scholar's Hall or Study. Here, I stop and notice where I am and what's around me—smells, sights, sounds. I ask myself, "Am I in synch with the true rhythm of this moment?" And what is that rhythm, you might ask? For me, it's the pace of nature itself, the rhythmic flow of the universe which, most of the time, is moving at a very different speed than what my hurried mind superimposes upon it.

Put simply, I know I'm one with this rhythm when I'm still enough to feel the moment as myself.

Trees, plants, and flowers radiate stillness. They silently beckon us to slow down and notice the presence in them, and in ourselves.

Within the Scholar's Courtyard, the still presence inherent in plants and trees abounds. Planted on the courtyard's southeast side are pink, white, and yellow peonies. The springtime counterpart of the plum, the peony (*mudan*) symbolizes nobility and rank, and is called the King of Flowers in China. Against the west wall, a lace maple (*feng*) provides shade in summer and a beautiful collage of orange-and-yellow leaves in autumn. Beneath the maple is rohdea (*wannianqing*), a green tongue-like plant with red berries. Also called Ten-thousand Years Green because of its hardiness, it symbolizes ten-thousand years of good fortune. Rohdea is often presented as a wedding gift, and when new businesses begin. High overhead, pink-and-white fan-shaped flowers wave in summer breezes from branches of the silk tree (*hehuan*) while, on the west side of the Scholar's Study porch, a camellia japonica (*shancha*) blooms with hot-pink flowers in January. And across the courtyard from the camellia, a plum tree (*mei*), which also blooms in winter despite the harsh cold, is a symbolic reminder that we too can blossom even under difficult circumstances.

In our garden, plum blossoms open not only on the tree—they also bloom under our feet in a plum-blossom-on-cracked-ice design set with pebbles into the Scholar's Courtyard floor. A popular motif in Chinese art, this angular pattern portrays lake ice breaking up in spring inset with stylized plum blossoms lying on the ice. The design moves us to pause and ponder: despite all our plans, how often do we find ourselves landing, like plum blossoms, wherever the wind decides?

*The ancient masters, who could compare with them?*
*They stepped through life lightly and carefully,*
*as if they were walking on ice.*

*– Laozi*

Snow is falling as I write this. Beneath the plum tree, a large upright stone softens beneath a fluffy mantle of white. Visually following the rock upwards, from bottom to top, is like climbing a snowcapped peak. Everything is hushed. A chill breeze stirs. Are these flakes falling in the mountains or in the city?

# Stone/*shi*
# Daoist Principle: *yin & yang*

*I set out looking for stones in the mountains,*
*and to my amazement found mountains*
*in the stones.*

*– Wumen*

As I've already noted, the garden is inseparable from the Chinese art of landscape painting. And Chinese landscape painting is inseparable from mountains. You might say that without mountains there would be no garden. Bringing mountains into the city is what makes a Chinese garden possible. And in order to do this, you're going to need two things: plenty of stones, and a lot of money to extract and transport them.

But not just any stone. In order to build an individual peak or mountain range (*jia shan*), you want large stones with a wild and weathered quality about them. Taihu stones (*taihushi*), chiseled from the bed of Lake Tai near Portland's sister city of Suzhou, are one type of stone that Chinese artisans have used for centuries to build these urban peaks. Taihu rock is soft limestone naturally formed by wind and lake-water movement. Over time, wind and waves work together to create flowing and fantastic shapes shot through with cracks, fissures, and holes. Taihu stones are often referred to as "the music of the universe" because wind can occasionally be heard humming or whistling through their open spaces, much like breath blowing through a flute.

> *How like these stones we are—*
> *worn away by the winds and waves of change*
> *until a breath deeper than our own*
> *moves through us and we sing.*

T aihu rock is heavy and solid. But in our garden (where nothing is as it appears) the individual stones are mounted so the heaviest end is at the top, and the lightest or narrowest end is at the bottom. This makes them look as though they defy gravity. Seemingly weightless, they resemble drifting clouds. Put this all together and we have stones that are heavy but light, hard yet soft. They unify opposites, what Daoists call balancing *yin* and *yang*.

In Chinese philosophy, *yin* and *yang* govern everything from personal and collective history, to medicine and diet. Originally, *yang* meant the sunny side of a mountain; *yin* the shady side. *Yin* is the cosmic feminine energy; *yang* the cosmic masculine.

What's important to remember is that, in the Chinese mind, *yin* and *yang* aren't separate. They're actually one energy with two different charges. Think of lovers passionately locked in the oneness of a sexual embrace. There's a co-creative, energetic tension in that activity—not conflict, but tension. Chinese philosophy postulates that it's this ongoing cosmic tension between receptive *yin* and assertive *yang* charges that ceaselessly gives birth to the world of complementary opposites you and I inhabit, and are inhabited by— birth and death, dark and light, back and front. You breathe in, you breathe out. You can't have one or know one without the other. If you try to eliminate one of the opposites because you don't like it (health without sickness, for example) you're on the road to destroying a delicately balanced system of interconnected relationships.

*What's a wise man but an ignorant man's teacher?*

*What's an ignorant man but a wise man's student?*

*Until you realize this for yourself, you'll continue*

*to stumble and fall in life no matter how learned you are.*

*It's the primordial secret.*

*– Laozi*

## SOUND IS SILENCE

What is Laozi's primordial secret? Precisely this: that what appear to be opposites are, in fact, dependent upon and in relationship to one another. Take sound and silence, for example. In Daoism and in Buddhism, sound is silence that's become audible and returns to silence. Activity is stillness that's taken on movement and returns to stillness. Form is formlessness arising out of and disappearing back into itself. Our bodies are forms. Which implies what? That the flip side of who and what we are is this vast alive formlessness ceaselessly moving into and out of form. Quantum physicists are just now discovering what Buddhists and Daoists have long held to be true; namely, contrary to appearances, our world and the myriad things in it, including our bodies, aren't solid, but consist almost entirely of empty space.

*Form is formlessness. Formlessness is form.*

*– the Buddhist Heart Sutra*

The two are not two. They are two sides of the same coin, and so comprise an indivisible unity.

Reawakening to this emptiness as yourself is what many spiritual traditions call "dying before you die."

*The great spiritual falsehood?*
*That you have to wait until you die*
*to return to the Source.*

*The even greater falsehood?*
*That there's a you*
*separate from the Source*
*who needs to return at all.*

What are you dying to? Your identification with thinking as yourself. What are you being reborn as? The formless one life that is your primordial essence. Many spiritual practices can facilitate this rebirth. Using meditative movement such as *taijiquan* or *qigong* to work with the subtler and less dense form of *qi* energy in and around your body can open a doorway into the formless. Sitting meditation (which we'll talk about more when we reach the Scholar's Study) is another way to begin to experience yourself as the spaciousness within which thoughts occur, rather than the thoughts themselves. Or, at a most basic yet profound level, simply listening to silence whenever and wherever you can—not as something separate from yourself, but as who and what you are at the deepest level—can facilitate a shift from thinking to being.

Many visual elements in the garden exemplify what I'm talking about here. Perhaps the most beautiful and profound are the garden's leak windows.

S et into the garden's inner and outer walls are square tracery "leak windows" (*louchuang*), so named because they leak a bit of the view from one side to the other, thus making the garden feel larger than it really is. Layering views in this way also entices us to move into the scenic area we glimpsed through the tracery so we can experience it fully for ourselves.

Based on designs in a 17th century book entitled *The Craft of Gardens* (*Yuanye*) by Ji Cheng, each window silently beckons us to peer through it into the world that lies beyond. It invites us to enter the Beyond within.

But these windows appear to be doing even more than this. Similar to Taihu stone, leak windows are both solid and open. The solid is *yang*, the openness *yin*. You can touch the tracery (form), but you can also put your hand through it (formlessness). One reveals the other. Can you do the same?

## ZHONGYONG

L ife is an ongoing balancing act between *yin* and *yang* energies. Solid and open, heavy and light, hard and soft, our task is to bring the opposites into unity, to find the median or balancing point between the polarities that are always in flux. And each person has to find this fulcrum or "mean" (*zhongyong*) for themselves. No one can tell us precisely where it is because everyone's life circumstances are different. What remains the same for all of us, however, is change. The polarities continue to shift and, if we don't know how to maintain our balance, we'll find ourselves continually pulled off center.

I sometimes use the following scenario to describe what this is like for me:

*I'm standing with my left foot on the back of one horse, and my right foot on the back of another horse. The reins are in my hands, and the horses (which represent the polarities) are galloping. If I go rigid, I'm going to get thrown. But, if I can learn to move with the horses, I stand a better chance of maintaining my balance. Occasionally, a horse will veer off suddenly in a direction I couldn't have predicted. What I do then is try, as best I can, to flow with what is happening. If one or both horses throw me, I attempt, like a good martial artist, to fall well, thus incurring upon myself the least amount of spiritual, emotional, psychological and, perhaps, even physical injury.*

Learning how to skillfully ride life's horses requires finding the reins within ourselves. And finding the reins inside can be a whole lot easier if we've found a soulful space to inhabit outside. The garden is such a space, and at its heart is the Scholar's Study.

SCHOLAR'S STUDY

Located on the secluded north side of the Scholar's Courtyard, the Scholar's Study is more than just a building. It's a corporeal reminder that we all need solitude, sanctuary, and contemplative space. Our physical, psychological, emotional, and spiritual health requires a place where we can simply be; a space where, for half an hour or an hour each day, we can step aside, breathe deeply and, with the poet Si Kongtu, whisper softly to ourselves:

> *The ten-thousand affairs*
> *of the human world*
> *are not my affairs.*

The Scholar's Study is poetically named "Celestial Hall of Permeating Fragrance." As this name implies, the study was home to a variety of heavenly smells that might have included burning incense, brewing tea, and the fragrant aroma from a flower-scented pine-soot ink stick being ground against an ink stone.

The traditional term for a study in Chinese is *shuzhai*. *Shu* means "book," and *zhai*, among other things, means "fasting." The study was a place to fast from the cares of life and the world. Here, amid scroll paintings, silk-lined boxes filled with books, and the soothing sound of rain dripping onto the large green leaves of the banana plant (*ba jiao*) standing outside his window, the scholar might have read and contemplated the Chinese literary classics. It was also where he may have practiced what Daoists call "fasting the mind" or Chan meditation.

Chan is Chinese for the sanskrit word *dhyana*, which means "sitting meditation." Chan emerged as a syncretism of Daoism and Mahayana Buddhism and, by the Tang dynasty (618–907 CE), was widely practiced. In *The Selected Poems of Wang Wei*, translator David Hinton states that the famous Tang dynasty scholar, poet, and landscape painter Wang Wei was a Chan practitioner. Eventually, Chan made its way to Japan where it became Zen.

Hinton goes on to describe how Chan focused, not on religion, but on the early philosophical teachings of Laozi and his followers. It revived and re-established Dao not only as a way or path, but as a cosmological process whereby forms ceaselessly come into being (*yu*) and then pass away into nonbeing (*wu*). The spiritual task of a Chan practitioner was to reawaken to and then live naturally and consciously as this interdependent process, rather than as a mind-identified self or ego. And in old China, the most effective and time-honored way to do this was by becoming a forest hermit or mountain recluse.

Chan's popularity was due, in part, to how well it meshed with the Chinese rivers-and-mountains (*shanshui*) eremitical tradition that, by the 10th century, had linked wilderness with spirituality in the Chinese psyche.

Wilderness is a place of emptying. It's where life strips away everything that we're not. Spiritually speaking, wilderness symbolizes the wide-open spaciousness or awareness we spontaneously return to when our ego relinquishes resistance and control. It represents a state of unconditioned consciousness wherein we are at home being alone with the alone, and our eyes become everything they see. Stepping through Chan meditation's gateless gate into this empty-mind wilderness, we begin to see that the processes of consciousness and cosmos are identical. Our thoughts appear out of nothing, evolve, and disappear back into nothing in the same way traffic noise arises out of and dissolves into silence. Life beyond us unfolds the same as life within us because cosmos and consciousness are one.

*We sit facing one another*
*the mountain and I*
*until only the mountain remains.*

*– Li Bo*

Like the poet/scholar Li Bo (701–762 CE), the scholar-official often aspired to be a mountain hermit. But how do you do this when duty demands (and your tastes dictate) that you live as an urbanite? A garden was the answer. Within its walls, the scholar created a forested mountain wilderness in the city—and Chan was a way to embody that wilderness.

## FOUR PERFECTIONS

Chan influenced a scholar's artistic life as well, turning the arts into spiritual practices. Brush painting and calligraphy were often referred to as "painting-Chan" and "calligraphy-Chan." A Chan artist's ideal was to move as a force of nature, creating as freely and spontaneously as the universe itself. Chan practice transformed the artist into a conduit for cosmic energy, out of which painting, calligraphy, and seal (or chop) carving arose. Ideally, when a scholar-artist pressed brush tip to paper or a vermillion-inked chop seal onto a document or work of art, he was acting not from a personal center of identity, but as the ever-present formless still point from which forms emerge as the universe's ten-thousand things.

Calligraphy, brush painting, and seal carving comprised three of what were called the Four Perfections. The fourth perfection was composing and reciting (or chanting) poetry.

# Poetry/*shige*
# Daoist Principle: *pu*

*Poetry is the expression of the wishes*
*of the heart-mind.*

*– from the Shijing (100 BCE)*

P oetry is undervalued in our culture. Not so, however, in the garden where, in the words of the 10th century monk Wei Feng, "Poetic minds complete the greater elegance."

Unlike most Western verse, poetry in the garden tends to be concrete. The poet isn't standing apart from nature writing about it. He or she *is* nature speaking for itself. The poet channels the energy of natural vistas and landscapes in order to create *qi yun*, or energy rhythm. It's this energetic rhythm that a poet aims to instill in the reader. A Daoist poet uses scenery (*jing*) to evoke feeling (*qing*), rather than a lot of thinking about what the poem means.

*Scenery in a garden is done well when it moves the emotions.*

*– Ji Cheng*

Still, words are limited. They only represent that to which they point. At times, even for the most skilled poet, there are simply no words that can convey an experience. I'm thinking, in particular, of the Chinese poet Tao Yuanming (365-427 CE) who, after reveling one day in the natural wonders of mountains and lakes, picked up his brush, dipped it in ink, and wrote:

*I know in all of this lies the true meaning. I try to communicate it,*
*but I forget the words.*

Imagine, a poet who has forgotten words, the tools of his trade! Clearly, Tao Yuanming had an experience of life so deep and powerful that trying to come up with words to describe it eluded him. It's almost as if he's saying to us, "Poetry fails the least at expressing the inexpressible, but it still fails! If this is true for poetry, how much more so for words used in ordinary discourse! Once you've experienced the ultimate reality, what need have you of words? Forget them!"

Tao Yuanming's words echo those of Zhuangzi, seven-hundred years earlier:

*Once you get the fish, you no longer need the fish trap. Once you get the rabbit, you no longer need the snare. Once you get the meaning, you no longer need the words. Show me a man who has forgotten words so that I might have a word with him.*

What I hear Zhuangzi saying is that words can become traps. Then, in his last line, he seems to play with us by pointing to the paradox that he has to use words to remind us not to be ensnared by them! Words are the tools of communication. They're what we've been given to work with. But can you use these tools rather than being used by them? Don't trick yourself into believing that because you've attached a word or a meaning to something you know what it is.

### SEE THROUGH THE MEANINGS

*De yi* literally means "get the meaning or idea" in Chinese. But, according to professor and author Hans-Georg Moeller, it's more often used to mean "get satisfaction" or "to be satisfied." In order to get satisfaction from life, do we first need to learn how to be satisfied with life *as it is*? Do mountains and lakes have meaning? Or are they simply what they are? The Daoist admonition "No ideas!" (*wu yi*) is meant to liberate us from our preoccupation with meanings by waking us up to the fact that our thoughts and ideas *about* reality are not reality itself, any more than an image or photo of a pine tree is the pine tree.

A teaching in Daoism called the Rule of Three goes like this:

*In the beginning, a mountain is a mountain, and water is water. Then, a mountain is no longer a mountain, and water is no longer water. Finally, a mountain is a mountain again, and water is again water.*

When we first see a mountain or lake we think we perceive it as it truly is. Then, as we reawaken to the Dao, we become aware of all the concepts, memories, expectations, ideas, and beliefs we project onto everything we see. We begin to realize that we no longer see mountains and water as they are, but *as we think they are.*

Finally, when this conceptual veil is removed from our mirror-mind, the mountain is again a mountain and water is again water. But now they're vibrant and pulsing with life because they're free of the projections that can deaden our felt experience of them.

*Our thoughts and ideas about reality are not reality itself.*

*Take a moment and notice your breathing. Breathing in, breathing out. Breathing is intimately connected to your body, which is always in the present moment no matter how your mind pushes and pulls it around.*

*Now, with relaxed alert attention, move deeper into your bodily sensations as you breathe. See if you can be your breathing rather than the "you" in your head noticing it. Close your eyes and do this for about twenty seconds.*

What did you notice? Perhaps, for a few seconds at least, you were aware that no thoughts arose. Using your breath as an anchor to your body liberated you from being pulled down the thought freeway in your head. Or, maybe you were thinking a lot. Either way, this raises the question: How can there be awareness of thought or no thought? Thinking can think about thinking, but it can't watch itself thinking about thinking. In short, it can't be aware of itself. This is because thought is the subject, and it's impossible for a subject to become its own object, in the same way that a fire can't burn itself and a fork can't stab itself. So how could you notice you were thinking or not thinking?

What I'd like to suggest is this: just as there can't be flight without space or sky, so too you can't be aware of thinking or not thinking without the larger Reality we might call pure consciousness or awareness. Realizing you are the limitless spacious sky, rather than your flights of mind, is what Buddhists call enlightenment. It's the Beyond within you.

*Now shift your attention to something nearby. It could be an object of any kind. Bring a relaxed alert awareness to it, and see if you can notice it without labeling or naming it. Can you simply observe it without wanting or not wanting it, liking it or not liking it? Can you let it speak for itself without judging or comparing it in any way?*

What did you experience? Was the exercise easy or difficult? If you're like me, you probably found it hard not to name or label what you were looking at. We've been conditioned from birth to put everything into a conceptual box as soon as we see it so we can move on to the next thing. And as soon as we slap a label onto something, be it an object or another human being, we lose touch with the truth of it. We drain life of its vitality every time we turn what's in front of us into an abstraction in our heads.

## A COMPLETE AND TOTAL MYSTERY

The East Indian sage, Krishnamurti, once said that as soon as you tell a child a bird is a bird, the child will never see the bird again. What they will see is the word "bird" in their head.

What we might be telling our children instead is, "We *call* this a bird" so we can communicate about it. The truth is we really don't know what it is. It's a complete and total mystery. And practicing the Daoist principle of *pu* can keep us vibrantly alive and open to that mystery.

*Realizing you are the limitless*
*spacious sky, rather than your flights of mind,*
*is what Buddhists call enlightenment.*

*Pu* in Chinese means "simplicity," but not simple as in stupid or simplifying life by downsizing our possessions. *Pu* is the simplicity that comes when we live life directly, when we see things as they are. Seeing things as they are (or seeing them in their suchness, to use the Buddhist term) occurs when we stop projecting our thoughts onto everything and everyone we meet, and then believing what we project. In Daoism, the metaphors for *pu* are the uncarved block and the undyed silk, which both symbolize our original state. Undyed silk isn't colored by beliefs, ideas, and opinions. An uncarved block is undifferentiated oneness before it manifests into multiplicity. The more we embody the *pu* of the uncarved block and the undyed silk, the simpler our lives become.

*Pu* is essential in Daoist poetry, which refrains from a lot of word manipulation, abstraction, and mind interference so life can speak for itself. It also plays an important role in a word game called capping or collaging lines (*jiju*), in which Chinese scholars challenged one another's literary skill by coming up with spontaneous, two-line poetic couplets (*duilian*). Someone would improvise the first line of a poem and someone else had to extemporize a second line. Sounds easy, but don't be deceived. This second line had to have the same number of characters and the same word order, or syntax, as the first. It also needed to create a parallelism with the previous line. Like the garden itself, the two lines created a lyrical, harmonious, and balanced world. They framed the Beyond within.

Here's an example of a couplet from inside the Scholar's Study. The first line hangs from a column on the right, the second from a column on the left:

> *Ten-thousand flowers bravely blossom in the snow.*
> *One tree leads the world welcoming the spring.*

The "one tree" is the plum, planted outside the Study. Notice in the couplet how numbers, plants, and seasons are used to create a parallel effect:

ten-thousand/one

flowers/tree

snow/spring

As you can imagine, capping lines was an art that demanded immense linguistic skill. But it also required the simplicity that comes from living life directly. The mind would love to take five minutes to come up with a really clever second line to complete the couplet, but there wasn't time. The game requires us to move as spontaneously as the Dao itself, in the same way as when wind blows across a lake the ripples don't wait to appear. They do so immediately. Or, when we clap our hands together the sound doesn't wait to come out.

*Simple in thought and behavior, you re-realize the source of being.*

*– Laozi*

THE LANGUAGE OF THE HEART

Speaking spontaneously from the heart is a challenge in a culture like ours that so thoroughly trains us in left-brain, linear thinking. But life is not a straight line from A to B. No matter how efficient our minds think this is, it's not how nature works. Life flows, curves, meanders. We allude to this when we say, "Life threw me a curve." Our human mind doesn't like curves because they don't provide a clear view of what's coming next. Curves create uncertainty which the mind fears, and so is constantly trying to avoid.

Poetry, on the other hand, is the language of the heart. Like life, it is non-linear and loves curves. *The Classic of Poetry* (*Shijing*) compiled in China about 100 BCE states that, "Poetry is the expression of the wishes of the heart -mind." According to scholar David Hinton, classical Chinese uses the same word for both "heart" and "mind." *Mind* refers to a clear mind mirroring things as they are, and *heart* is the felt experience of this clear seeing. Poetry, therefore, is the spiritual desire of our heart-mind (*xin*) to experience and express what we see and feel as one.

For the scholar, poetry wasn't a frill. It was an essential element in an artistic and spiritual life support system that centered him within the great Way or Dao no less than sitting meditation or *taijiquan*. Composing and reciting poetry was one of the arts through which the scholar expressed his moral values and distilled life's elemental truths.

In the garden, these truths are poetically and symbolically embodied by our final element: plants.

# Plants/*zhiwu*
# Daoist Principle: *de*

*If a home is without a garden and an old tree,*
*from where, I ask you, will the joys in life come?*

*– Chen Haozi*

L eaving the Scholar's Study we head west through a doorway, and then meander south along a path past blooming pink hibiscus and vibrant red Seville roses until we reach the Flowers Bathing in Spring Rain Pavilion. Rectangular in shape, this pavilion could double as a waterside stage when musical and theatrical events were performed for the scholar, his family, and guests who gathered to watch or listen.

The name "Flowers Bathing in Spring Rain" reminds me how we can wash away disharmony and imbalance by using flora and fauna as models for how to live our lives well. The bamboo, for instance—it's very strong, but can bend in the wind without breaking. Can you be strong yet flexible like the bamboo in your daily life? Or the quintessential floral symbol in Buddhism is the lotus flower (*hehua*). Rooted in the lake mud, the lotus rises about twenty-four inches above the water where it puts out an incredible bloom. There's a saying in Buddhism:

*Let us live like the lotus,*
*at home in the muddy water,*
*opening to life as it is.*

People sometimes think this little aphorism points to indifference and passivity, but it doesn't. As you may know from personal experience, turning the muddy water in your life into that flower, again and again, is anything but passive.

This saying also hearkens back to Buddhist cosmology which teaches that, because all things arise together, nothing exists by itself separate from everything else. Opening to life as it is connotes acceptance of the fact that it has taken the activity of the entire universe to bring this moment into being. You can argue with the form this moment takes, but by the time you're arguing with it, it already is what it is. It's a done deal, which makes arguing with it futile.

In the Disney movie, *Mary Poppins*, the father, Mr. Banks, insists that the new nanny, Mary Poppins, teach his two children to engage life the way he does—as a battle to be fought. Apparently, Mr. Banks' ego-driven, militaristic approach to life doesn't come naturally, so children must be taught to live this way. Left to their natural inclinations, it would probably never occur to them to live life in such an antagonistic and unhealthy manner.

Like Mr. Banks, most of us have been conditioned to believe it's our human duty to struggle and fight against life. Otherwise, how will our ego get what it wants? Consequently, we suffer from living in a state of internal and external resistance to how things actually are and to how life is unfolding. The Daoist sage (*zhenren*), on the other hand, knows the deeper current of life carries us away whether we fight against it or not, and so has stopped struggling. A Daoist master doesn't resist the waves of life— she rides them like a surfer. Our level of inner peace will depend on whether or not we can do the same.

## PERFECT ACTION

Accepting what is or what was doesn't mean I condone abuse or deny hurtful things that happened to me. It means I accept that what happened happened and move on, thus freeing myself of if onlys, what ifs, and all my paralyzing mental lists of what others should or shouldn't have done that obscure the moment by trapping me in past and future.

Nor does acceptance mean I can't take action in response to what's happening. What I'm talking about here is not inaction, but *perfect action* that arises out of acceptance of what is. Acceptance enables me to respond to the moment as the moment rather than as my thinking, judging mind. In short, acceptance doesn't separate me from and pit me against the moment the way non-acceptance does. And what, I ask you, is more likely to help me deal in a skillful, healing way with what's going on? A *reaction* that addresses what's happening from a place of divisiveness, resistance, and fighting against? Or a *response* that arises out of a genuine connection to what's actually taking place?

I recently received two mailings. One was from a US presidential candidate. The other came from a group dedicated to defending the US Constitution. What stood out for me in both communiqués was their use of words. In the presidential hopeful's letter, there were no less than fifteen references to fighting for or against something. The second letter contained fourteen references to attacks, assaults, battles, and fights.

*Like and don't like, for and against.*
*This is the primal disease of the human mind.*

*– Sengcan*

Could opening to life the way flowers do cure the disease that the 6th century Chinese sage, Sengcan, is talking about? If so, then our final Daoist principle, *de* (pronounced "deh"), is a way to effect this cure in day-to-day life.

In Chinese, *de* means "virtue," but not virtue in a moral sense. Originally, the ancient Chinese character for *de* depicted a farmer tilling fields. The *de* or virtue of the field is its ability to raise crops. Later, this ideogram was combined with the character depicting a foot stepping forward. Together, these characters mean "virtue in action" or "virtue stepping into the world."

I like to imagine that the *de* of a flower bathing in spring rain is its innate ability to open to what is. This means the flower blooms regardless of the weather. If the weather is what we call good, it opens. If it's what we call bad, it opens too.

Like a flower, the *de* or virtue of a human being is our ability to bloom—not only *in* the world, but *as* the world. And blooming often involves risk. People around you may not understand or like what they see flowering. Consequently, relationships could end, a job might be lost, and long-held beliefs may go by the wayside. You might be wrapping up your law degree, only to rediscover that what you've always felt called to do is open a painted rock shop at the beach.

But where you live and what you do for a living are relatively small matters compared to re-realizing and then bringing who and what you truly are—along with your unique character and gifts—into being. What you call your life is actually the universe's one shot at doing this, and if it's lost it's lost forever. The great 20th century German poet Rainer Maria Rilke called this the "Great Work" that, sadly, is often left undone because our tendency is to let society's ego-driven values distract us from being our deepest and truest self.

### APPLYING THESE PRINCIPLES IN DAY-TO-DAY LIFE

I can imagine someone reading this book may think: "Well, these Daoist principles are all fine and dandy, but how am I supposed to apply them in a culture that's traveling one-thousand miles per hour in the opposite direction?" It's a good question, one I've wrestled with frequently. Speaking from my own experience, here's what I've found out.

I hold these principles and apply them whenever and wherever I can, knowing that, at times, I'm going to have to jump through societal hoops and play the cultural game. Hopefully, however, I'll know I'm playing the game when I play it. It seems most of our society isn't aware there's a game going on at all. And, from where I stand, the game looks something like this: I am what I think. I am what I do. I am my roles. I am what I possess ... and so on.

To the extent I identify with any or all of these as who and what I am, I'm unwittingly setting myself up for suffering. This is because my thoughts, roles, occupations, possessions, and the like are forms, which are always in a state of flux. They arise and they dissolve. A relationship ends. The firm downsizes and I lose my job. My health falls apart. I discover you aren't who I thought you were, or I'm not who I thought I was. You name it.

Our culture tells me I should be able to line up all my ducks in a row on the table and keep them there, but life doesn't work that way. Life is impermanent. Eventually, something (or everything) is going to fall off the table onto the floor. And if I'm identified solely with what falls I'm going to fall with it. Whereas, if I've reawakened to the formless one life as who and what I am, then forms can come and go. I can play with them freely and without expectation because I'm not attaching my sense of self to what can't possibly last. Beneath the inevitable pain of loss there's what's been called "the peace that's beyond all understanding."

*It's no easy thing for a principle to become a person's own*
*unless it be maintained and worked out, each day,*
*in his or her life.*

*– Epictetus*

## THE LAKESIDE TERRACE

From the Flowers Bathing in Spring Rain Pavilion, it's a short stroll west over the Double Rainbow Covered Bridge to the lakeside terrace adjoining the Lotus Hall.

Looking north from this terrace, the scene opens onto an expansive vista that takes in all of the garden's five elements: the water of Qin Lake; the architecture of the Painted Boat in Misty Rain Pavilion and the Tower of Cosmic Reflections teahouse; the Ten-thousand Ravines in Thick Clouds miniature mountain range, built entirely of Lake Tai rock; a couplet mounted on two columns in the Moon-Locking Pavilion; and, on a summer day, lotus flowers rising out of the lake.

*From the Lakeside Terrace of the Lotus Hall*

*I tuck scented verses*
*into the lotus blossoms.*

*What you smell are these words*
*wafting from a stamen's stanza.*
*What you feel is a stem's*
*single-syllable line*
*swaying you in the breeze.*

*Like bees among petals,*
*poems enter the body.*
*What you gather*
*from the open flower of this place*
*pollinates everything you touch.*

*You leave here,*
*fluent in the cursive script of fish.*
*Your breath sings like wind*
*through a thousand*
*rain-soaked pines.*

*What people glimpse*
*in your eyes now*
*is a lake too clear to name;*
*a view from pinnacled peaks*
*that's older than birth or death.*

The *qin* (Chinese zither) is an ancient stringed instrument dating back nearly three-thousand years. Often played to accompany the chanting of poems, many poets and scholars were accomplished *qin* players. The famous Tang dynasty (618–907 CE) poet, Li Bo, recounts in one of his poems how a skilled *qin* player was able to recreate the sound of cold wind sighing through a thousand pines just by plucking a single string. Over time, this instrument became a symbol of the scholar's achievement and status.

Stand long enough on the garden's lakeside terrace, and you might see how Qin Lake got its name. Watch quietly. Growing next to the Painted Boat in Misty Rain Pavilion is a willow tree. Wait for a breeze. Can you see how the tips of the willow's long lithe branches strum ripples across the water's surface?

PAINTED BOAT IN MISTY RAIN

You stand on the prow of a boat as mist drifts over the lake. Through bare tree branches, light from a full autumn moon shimmers across the water. Lamplight from your boat flickers in lake ripples like stars. A chill breeze touches your cheek. Dried willow leaves swirl and skitter across the deck. From somewhere in the garden, the haunting sound of notes being played on a two-stringed *erhu* drift out upon the night air. Inspired, you grind some ink, take out a brush and, unrolling a fresh sheet of rice paper, write the following couplet:

> *Disappearing into the fog, who can say where the erhu's song is heading?*
> *Appearing out of the mist, who knows where the fisherman's boat has been?*

In China, a fisherman represents the recluse or hermit. By association, boats are symbols of a secluded life lived away from the cares and pressures of the human world. Chinese paintings frequently portray a lone figure in a boat winding along a river through high mountains. Where's the figure in the boat going? Where have they been? We don't know. Who the figure is and why they are where they are remains hidden from our view. Chinese artists use mist or haze in their work to heighten this air of mystery.

For me, the Painted Boat in Misty Rain Pavilion has always been wrapped in a similar haze of unanswerable questions. Is the boat embarking or disembarking? Or, like life, is it doing both at the same time? We say my ship has come in when good fortune smiles on us. But wait long enough and, like that ship, it will soon be heading off toward the horizon. In any given moment, isn't there as much pulling into our lives as there is pulling out?

116

During the Ming dynasty, the Painted Boat (or Boat Hall) was a place to relax and catch any cool breezes rising off the lake on a hot summer day. It may have also served as a meeting place for a romantic twilight rendezvous. It's said that Lan Su Yuan's painted boat is "a boat filled with friendship, sent from the people of Suzhou to the people of Portland." Isn't this the kind of vessel we'd all like to see pulling up to our dock? Doesn't a boat filled with cargo like this make life's partings a little more bearable?

## TEN-THOUSAND RAVINES IN THICK CLOUDS

Rising up inside the garden's north wall is the Ten-thousand Ravines in Thick Clouds miniature mountain range. Throughout cultures, mountains have long been sacred connections between earth and heaven. No less so in China, where mountains are the cloud-wrapped abodes of hermits and Daoist Immortals. Wandering these ancient heights, you might happen upon the stone hut of a recluse or stumble into "cave heaven," an enchanted peaceful place, free from time, where everyone and everything is at one with the Dao.

I've long wished that guests could enter the garden from behind this mountain range. Picture, if you will, what it would be like to catch glimpses of the garden through fissures and holes in the Lake Tai rock on your way in. Imagine how sounds from the waterfall tumbling over rocks in the grotto on the opposite side would increase your desire to be inside, or how the heavenly scent of lotus blossoms wafting through the rocky openings would entice you onward. Like the old fisherman in the story *Peach Blossom Spring*, you'd find yourself being drawn toward the reality that another world does, indeed, lie beyond. You'd be longing to experience the Beyond within.

The Tower of Cosmic Reflections is a two-story building or tower (*louge*) that overlooks Qin Lake. Peering down through one of the ornately framed second-story windows, you might glimpse these cosmic reflections captured in the mirror-like surface of the water. I like to imagine the poetic name "cosmic reflections" may also refer to the expansive insights that can come when we reflect on life from a cosmic, rather than an egoic perspective.

In the Ming dynasty the tower's upper story could be a gathering place for the women of a literati family. Today, both floors serve as the garden's teahouse. Here, amid beautiful antique Qing furniture and the watery sounds of music played on the *guzheng* (a zither larger than the *qin*), you can sip tea from all over China, as well as partake of a light lunch or snacks.

ONE TASTE

In China it's said, "Tea and Dao are one taste." This is another way of saying that tea is the Dao in disguise. When you get right down to it, though, *everything* is the Dao in disguise—and a regular tea practice is one way to taste this truth for yourself.

*Cha Dao* (the Way of tea) and the garden are a powerful duo that can nurture this realization in several ways.

Like the garden, tea invites us to slow down. It refocuses us by drawing our scattered attention back to what's right in front of us. Popular advertising slogans like "Tea on the go!" reduce tea to a mere beverage. They pull tea out of its larger contemplative and social context, and so rob it of its power to raise consciousness and bring people together.

"Drink tea, make friends" is an old Chinese proverb. In our modern world, most of us confuse electronic social media with a face-to-face social life. Our ability to be fully present to someone—or ourselves—without an electronic gadget constantly distracting us is fast becoming a lost art. The cure? Slow down, turn off whatever beeps, rings, or vibrates, and invite someone to tea.

Properly preparing and drinking tea can reawaken you to the present moment, or the Now. Silence your cell phone, center yourself, and notice what's right in front of you. Past and future are going on only in your head. Vapor rising from your teapot is Now. The tree standing outside the teahouse window is Now. Tea and pot are both Now. The Now is not only what's brewing, it's also the space within which it's brewing.

Similar to the garden, a tea practice surrounds us with all the splendors of non-human nature. Everything we touch, hear, see, smell, and taste while practicing the art of tea is designed to awaken us to our oneness with the natural world. The cups and pot, for instance, are ideally earthenware, while the drain board on which our tea is prepared is usually crafted from bamboo. Take time to feel them. The sound of water pouring from kettle to pot transports us to a small waterfall trickling over stones high in the mountains. Steeping leaves release an aroma not unlike the smell of warm summer rain seeping through dried pine needles carpeting a forest floor. Swirling steam curls and vanishes like fog drifting through ancient trees. And our first sip is nothing less than the universe blooming on our tongue. Again, the line between inner and outer is blurred. What was outside is now inside. Or was it ever really outside to begin with?

*G*ongfu in Chinese means "art" or "skill." As such, *gongfu* tea is the art of preparing, serving, and drinking tea. Look closely and you'll see that the elements in a Chinese garden and those in a *gongfu* tea ceremony are one and the same.

First, we have plants, in this case the camellia sinensis (*chashu*), from which tea is harvested. Next comes water, in which the leaves are steeped. Alongside these we have poetry, which has shared the tea table in China for centuries. Countless Chinese poems have been inspired by tea, and many pieces of teaware (especially teapots) have lines from famous poems inscribed into them. The stones in the garden, which represent earth or mountains, share a relationship with *yixing* clay (pronounced "ee-shing"), from which many of the small teapots used for *gongfu* tea are made. And finally, there's the garden teahouse itself, which is the element of architecture. True, you don't need a teahouse to practice the art of tea. But, if you practice the art well, wherever you are will become a tea abode within which you can glimpse the entire cosmos reflected in your cup.

## THE HUT BENEATH THE PINE

*T*here's a wonderful quote by the 14th century Japanese court composer, Toyohara Sumiaki, who wrote:

*Tea is a place to escape to when you can't ease your cares in the mountains.*
*Tea is the hut beneath the pine in the midst of the city.*

Sumiaki's words point to a longstanding connection between tea and the secluded life of a Daoist sage or hermit. The hut beneath the pine is where such a recluse lived, and tea is a "way" to find that hut, even amid the hustle and bustle of the city.

## MOON-LOCKING PAVILION

Situated near the center of Qin Lake, the Moon-Locking Pavilion is an open-air, hexagonal structure accessed from both east and west by a granite zigzag bridge. With its blue-gray, pinnacled tile roof, this pavilion looks like a small mountain rising from the water. It also resembles a hermit's thatched-roof bamboo hut.

This semblance to both hut and mountain could be a visual reference to "Thatch-Hut Mountain," famous in China for its connection to the rivers-and-mountains poetry tradition, and also for poet Tao Yuanming who lived on the mountain's northwestern slopes.

In Chinese landscape poetry, the verb *suo* (meaning "to lock") is often used to convey the sense of capturing a scene or image. Isn't this what we do when we create a painting or take a photograph? We are, in essence, trying to lock in or preserve in perpetuity that scene or moment.

Similarly, on certain months, this pavilion "locks" or embraces the full moon reflected in the water within its own reflection. This creates a lovely dark-and-light, *yin/yang* effect on the surface of the lake. To a keen observer, the moon's reflection is also that which is beyond appearing within.

I n the same way that the moon waxes toward fullness then wanes, so all things begin and come to an end. In each new beginning are the seeds of an ending; in each ending, the seeds of the next beginning.

I like to end my tours with a tale that, like the Moon-Locking Pavilion, beautifully captures or "locks in" my garden experience—the story of *The Magic Gourd*. The gourd I refer to is a bottle gourd. Shaped like an hourglass, a gourd's rounded top represents heaven; the bottom, earth. Used by Daoist healers to carry herbal remedies and elixirs of immortality, gourds were believed to possess magical properties. Over time, practitioners of Chinese medicine adopted the gourd as a symbol for an energy center called the lower *dantian* (or "field of the elixir") located about three inches below the navel. And in Daoism the gourd is a metaphor for the undifferentiated Dao with all the seeds of multiplicity and potentiality waiting inside it.

A gourd is one small vessel filled with many meanings, and probably as many stories. One version of the gourd story that I like goes like this:

*An old Daoist herb seller known as the gourd man sat relaxing behind his market stall at the end of a long day, and on the ground in front of him stood a bottle gourd about two-hands high. The old man's attention was fixed so intently on the gourd that he didn't notice the market officer, Changfeng, glancing at him now and then from the next stall where he was sweeping. Sweep, glance. Sweep, glance. This went on a minute or two until, to Changfeng's amazement, he saw the gourd man stand up, jump toward the gourd, and disappear inside it!*

*Changfeng witnessed this same disappearing act re-enacted evening after evening. Unable to curb his curiosity any longer, Changfeng mustered his courage and at dusk the following day ventured behind the stall where the elderly man sat pondering the gourd. "Where are you going when you vanish into that gourd?" Changfeng asked nervously.*

*The gourd man only smiled and said, "Well, why don't you come with me and see?"*

*So they both jumped into the gourd, where they beheld splendor after natural splendor and wonder after wonder. One path led them through an ornately carved gate that opened into hanging gardens. Another road traversed hills covered with orchards in full bloom. Yet another led them to vistas of mountain ranges and waterfalls. And on and on they went, reveling in what's referred to in China as "all nature's wonders contained in this gourd heaven."*

Changfeng and the gourd man experienced a world within the gourd that extended far beyond the gourd's tiny, tiny space. Within the garden, we too can experience a world far beyond the parameters of the garden's one city block. As the gourd man invited Changfeng into the gourd, Lan Su Yuan invites us to enter, perhaps not so much another world, but *our own world* seen through awakened eyes. Stepping into Lan Su's gourd heaven we enter what's small and touch the eternal. We rediscover that the one heart of heaven and earth is nothing less than our own heart beating as the Beyond within.

# FREQUENTLY ASKED QUESTIONS

*When was Lan Su Yuan built, and by whom?*

Ideas for the garden began in the 1980s. Construction began in mid 1998, and the garden opened its doors on September 14, 2000.

The garden was designed by Mr. Kuang Zhenyan who led design teams from the Suzhou Institute of Landscape Architecture Design, in cooperation with Portland colleagues, in blending Ming dynasty construction methods and contemporary building codes to build the garden. Many parts of our garden were constructed, dismantled, crated up, and shipped from Suzhou to Portland where teams of Chinese artisans reassembled everything, very much like a jigsaw puzzle. They used no nails—buildings were constructed using dovetailed, mortise and tenon joinery. Wooden pegs were used where needed. In addition, five-hundred tons of stone were shipped from China for use in our garden.

*Whose idea was it to build a Chinese garden here? Who paid for the garden?*

In 1985, Portland City Commissioner Mike Lindberg, accompanied by Oregon State Congressman David Wu, made a trip to Fuzhou in Fujian province to discuss a possible sister-city relationship. On their way home, David suggested he and Mike stop at Suzhou, David's ancestral home. Mike was entranced with Suzhou, especially with Suzhou's gardens. From that time forward, Commissioner Lindberg's focus shifted from Fuzhou to a Portland/Suzhou sister-city relationship with a Suzhou-style garden as its centerpiece.

In 1993, Portland Mayor Vera Katz, along with local businessman Bill Naito, procured the donation of land for the garden (estimated at 1.5 million dollars) from Northwest Natural. The Portland Development Commission raised nearly 5.5 million dollars, and the remainder of the funds came from private donations, businesses, and foundations.

*Who owns the garden?*

The City of Portland owns the physical structures in the garden, but Northwest Natural owns the land, which it leased to the City of Portland for ninety-nine years for $1. The garden is managed by Lan Su Chinese Garden, formerly known as Portland Classical Chinese Garden, a 501(c)(3) nonprofit organization established solely to operate the garden.

*How large is the garden?*

The garden is one city block. It measures about forty-thousand square feet, or a little less than one acre.

*What size would a garden have been during the Ming dynasty?*

A garden could have been larger or smaller than Lan Su Yuan, depending on the wealth of the family. Such gardens were located in the midst of the city where land was at a premium, and so were typically small. Most of Suzhou's gardens range from one to nearly thirteen acres in size.

*Were scholars' gardens public or private?*

Typically, they were private gardens used by the scholar and his extended family, although gardens were occasionally opened to the public on festival days. The literati frequently visited each other's gardens in the same way that English aristocrats visited one another's estates.

*Where is Suzhou located? What's the climate like compared to Portland?*

Suzhou is located about fifty miles west of Shanghai in the Yangtze River delta area. The climate is about ten degrees warmer than Portland on average. It's hotter and more humid in the summer, and wetter. It does snow occasionally, but the winters are milder than ours.

*Are there still gardens in Suzhou?*

Yes—but wars, rebellions, and the Cultural Revolution in the 1960s took their toll on many. The gardens were built for an elite class, and so for the Communists were symbols to be destroyed. It's conjectured there may have been as many as four-hundred fifty gardens in the Suzhou area prior to the Cultural Revolution; afterwards, there were around sixty. Gardens now open to the public include: The Humble Administrator's Garden, The Lingering Garden, The Master of Nets Garden, The Canlang Pavilion, The Lion Grove Garden, The Garden of Cultivation, and The Couple's Garden Retreat. Eight of these are now UNESCO World Heritage Sites.

*What was the prototype for a garden like this?*

The earliest known prototype for Chinese gardens goes back to the Spring and Autumn Period in China (770–476 BCE). The imperial hunting grounds (*yuanyou*) were partly cultivated and partly wild. A tall column called a *lingtai* was erected here so that the ruler, the son of heaven, could ascend it and commune with the deities. This combination of vegetation with architecture set the stage for the garden as we know it today. Poetry and landscape painting were also major influences in the evolution of garden design.

*What was Daoism like during the Ming dynasty?*

According to Daoism scholar Eva Wong, religious Daoism in the Ming dynasty (1368–1644) had branched into a variety of schools, one of which was Magical Daoism, or the Way of Power. Daoist magicians were individuals who could reputedly harness the energies of nature to achieve certain outcomes. Sorcerers, on the other hand, were adept at accessing the world of deities and spirits, much like their shamanic predecessors. The Ming rulers were trying to re-establish Chinese rule after overthrowing the Mongols. Clearly, Magical Daoism, with its emphasis on power, was seen by Ming leaders as a way to reestablish and secure control in a time of vibrant change, expansion, and great uncertainty.

*How did something as opulent as the garden mesh with Daoist and Confucian values and principles?*

That's a good question—especially since neither Daoism nor Confucianism condoned riches and ostentatious shows of wealth.

The first way to resolve this dilemma was to incorporate mountains, rivers, and forests into a garden, thus demonstrating that the scholar was a lover of nature. Daoists and Confucians revered nature, so this appeased both groups. Second, a garden was a soulful space where a healthy relationship to prestige and possessions could be cultivated. Ideally, envy, vice, and covetousness were converted into virtue and refinement, which were then reflected in the scholar's public service—all of which satisfied Confucian sensibilities. Next, the aesthetic in a scholar's garden was understated. Rather than using gold leaf and richly laminated ceramic surfaces, subtle earth tones were used, which silently said, "I'm refined and tasteful."

In essence, they were pretending it wasn't about money when it was. Transporting tons of rock to build a mountain range or traveling to far reaches of the country to bring back new cultivars of plants was incredibly expensive. Such acquisitions were ways of saying, "I'm rich," without saying it. Or as I recall hearing once in a talk on Chinese gardens, it was like saying, "Oh, that old thing!" (wink, wink) when guests praised your new jade carving that everyone knew cost a fortune.

*How did someone become a scholar?*

Status and prestige in old China didn't come with wealth. They came by obtaining a government position. This required passing the imperial examinations, which were open to any male nineteen years of age or older. Typically, scholars were educated from about age five to get very high scores on the exams, which conferred immediate social and political status, as well as a steady income. A scholar could continue to take advanced exams in order to secure promotions. This, of course, required a lifetime of ongoing study.

A grueling all-day-and-night affair, the examinations tested a scholar in the Confucian classics, which included history, geography, government, philosophy, poetry, and calligraphy.

*Were women in the literati class allowed to take the exams?*

No—but literati women could be highly educated by private tutors. They might become herbalists, playwrights, musicians, or published poets. They also usually ran the entire family estate and its finances while the scholar carried out his bureaucratic duties away from home. For a glimpse into the world of women during this period, I recommend the novel *Snowflower and the Secret Fan* by Lisa See.

*Where did the family sleep and prepare food?*

Living quarters (including kitchens and sleeping areas) were separate from (or adjacent to) a garden. They were sometimes accessed through a gate in the garden wall, but not always.

*How did they heat the buildings?*

In early China braziers were used to burn charcoal—think of a hibachi barbeque on legs. Also, the floors and walls could be covered in winter with tapestries. The family also wore thick, padded clothes. Small portable braziers were used as hand warmers.

*Did they use glass in the windows?*

No—window spaces were open or shuttered. Latticework in window spaces and doors was usually filled in with mica, silk, or oiled paper.

*What's the bluish-gray material on the roofs and on many of the walls, walkways, and floors?*

This is tile, made from yellow clay found in abundance in and around Suzhou. This clay is mixed with water, placed in molds, and then baked in a kiln fired with rice chaff for about forty days. The ash and smoke give the tile its bluish-gray color.

*What types of wood were used in the garden's construction?*

Inside, the beams and columns are imported China fir (*shanmu*). Pine (*song*) was used for some of the larger columns. Most of the light, blond-colored wood used for decorative carvings is gingko (*yinxing*), although cypress was used for this purpose in the Lounge Hall. Camphor (*zhangshu*) was used for balustrades on lakeside pavilions and in some roof rafters, while door and window panels are made from *nanmu* wood. Similar to walnut, *nanmu* really doesn't have an equivalent in the West. According to the Huntington Botanical Gardens in San Marino, California, *nanmu* comes from the laurel family, and is a protected species in China. As such, we are fortunate to have it used in our garden.

*There are symbols in bas-relief on triangular tiles that run along the roofline. What are they, and what do the symbols mean?*

These are bat-shaped "drip" tiles. The bat is a symbol of good fortune in China because the word bat (*fu*) is a homonym for blessing (*fu*).

In the upper right and left hand corners of each bat tile you'll see small gourds. The gourd (*hulu*) is a vessel for Daoist elixirs of immortality, and so is said to contain powerful spiritual energies. The central symbol is *shou* (pronounced: "show"), the character for long life. And flying around this *shou* symbol are five stylized bats, which represent the five blessings of health, wealth, virtue, longevity, and a peaceful death.

### Why do the rooflines on the buildings turn up at the ends?

We really aren't sure, but there are some possible reasons. On a practical level, the upturned roofline (called an "artichoke leaf" design) helps keep rain away from the sides and foundations of the buildings. It also lets in more light during winter, and less in summer. The roof ends could also represent unfurled bat or phoenix wings. The phoenix is a mythical bird that represents the Chinese empress and you'll often see the phoenix coupled with the dragon (the emperor) in Chinese art. Energetically, it's also believed the curved ends keep the *qi* energy flowing and from becoming stagnant.

### Why do paths and bridges in the garden zigzag and meander?

Our garden is designed to slow you down. A path that might normally take three steps to traverse, here takes nine or more. A zigzag path or bridge also makes you change direction a bit as you walk so you get a slightly different view with each step. Consider as well that, in Chinese folklore, it's said harmful spirits travel only in straight lines (quite a departure from the West, where straight lines are highly valued for speed and their so-called "efficiency"). By curving or zigzagging the pathways, it's believed you can deter these spirits from following you around.

### What are the two large stone creatures on the south side of the entry plaza?

These are guardian lions. The male is holding a cosmic ball and the female has her paw on a lion cub. The two are typically used together to guard a sacred space, and to balance out *yin/yang* energy.

Although the early Chinese didn't know what lions looked like (they're native to Africa), they'd heard about them, and how ferocious they could be, from merchants traveling the trade routes. The Chinese did know what dogs looked like, however, so they put the two together and came up with something that looks like both.

*What are the two dragon-like creatures facing each other on top of the Lotus Hall?*

These are called dragonfish (*chiwen*). It's believed they bring rain and protect buildings from fire. Reputedly, dragonfish can swim easily through harsh currents and choppy water. As such, they symbolize the endurance required to swim the choppy waters of life.

*There appear to be sculptures of potted plants on the roof below each dragonfish. What are they?*

Limbs laden with peaches emerge from a pot on the roof's south side to the right. The peach symbolizes longevity in China. On the left side of the roof another pot contains branches filled with pomegranates, symbolizing abundance, fertility, and the blessing of many sons. On the roof's north side you'll see a Buddha's hand citrus to the right, which symbolizes luck and happiness (*fo shou*), and on the left a blooming plum branch, symbolizing hope and endurance. Together, the peach, pomegranate, and Buddha's hand are called the Three Plenties.

*A swastika design recurs in the garden, especially in the tracery work along the upper part of the covered walkways. What does it mean?*

This is a reverse swastika. It's a good luck symbol that made its way into China along with Buddhism. Empress Wu (693 CE) declared the design to be the source of all auspiciousness, and gave it the pronunciation *wan*, a homophone on the Chinese word for "infinity" or "ten thousand." Ten thousand can refer to limitless blessings, but I like to think of the reverse swastika as being like the spinning blades of an energy fan. This fan pulls in positive energy and exhausts negative energy.

Energy (*qi*) in China is incredibly important. Everything radiates and attracts certain energies. As such, the color, shape, and placement of objects is key in creating positive and balanced energy flow. Chinese geomancy, which is the art and science of facilitating this flow, is known as *fengshui*, or "wind and water."

## *Were fengshui principles used when designing the garden?*

Yes. For example, the three formal buildings (Lotus Hall, Scholar's Study, and Tower of Cosmic Reflections) all have entryways that face south, which is the most auspicious direction for buildings to face since it provides more sunlight (*yang*). The Ten-thousand Ravines in Thick Clouds mountain range in the north provides shade (*yin*), as well as protection from wind and negative energy. Our garden is also built between the Willamette River to the east and Portland's west hills. This creates a balanced conjunction of sunlight (*yang*), shade (*yin*), hills (*yang*), and water (*yin*).

## *Tell me more about the lanterns inside the buildings and pavilions.*

Illuminated in early China by candles or oil, lanterns are often hexagonally shaped. Six, in China, is an auspicious number because the word for six (*liu*) sounds similar to the word for prosperity (*lu*). It therefore symbolizes promotion and rank. The angled lantern panels are often decorated with hand-written poems and paintings. In addition, red-and-gold tassels hang from each lantern. In China, red is the color for happiness, gold the color for good fortune. By creating a tassel in these colors, we have a constant flow of happiness and good fortune raining down on our heads.

## *What are the tall, pocked columnar formations that look like petrified wood?*

In China, these are called Shoot Stones (*shisun*) because they resemble bamboo shoots coming up out of the ground. Shoot stones are sedimentary rock, chiseled from cave floors in southeastern China. They are usually erected in trios, with the taller one in the center, because this formation resembles the Chinese character for mountain: 山. So, as you walk through the garden, notice where a mountain is represented, a forest, or a river. All these wild places are symbolically represented here so that in the midst of a city you can have mountains, rivers, and forests.

*What are the miniature potted forest scenes and mountainscapes called?*

The term for these miniatures is *penjing*, which literally means "landscape in a container." The Japanese word *bonsai* was taken from another Chinese word *penzai*, which means "potted plant."

*How many plants are there in the garden? Did they all come from China?*

There are approximately two-hundred twenty species in the garden. Because of quarantine restrictions, however, the majority of plants (with the exception of peonies) had to be found in the United States, most from the Pacific Northwest and West Coast.

# ACKNOWLEDGEMENTS

The poem on page 13 was first published in *Sufi* magazine under the title "The Beyond Within."

The excerpt on page 46 that begins "My window frames ancient mountains ..." is from a poem published in its entirety in *Manzou* (Daniel Skach-Mills, 2014) under the title: "Gazing at Ten-Thousand Ravines in Thick Clouds Through a Window in the Four-Sided Hall."

The quote on page 75, "a shaken bell tingling the air" was taken from the poem "Garnishmint" which was first published in *Bellowing Ark*. It was later reprinted in *In This Forest of Monks* (Daniel Skach-Mills, 2012).

The poems on pages 11, 48, 62, 77, and 88 were published in *The Tao of Now* (Ken Arnold Books, 2008).

Lan Su Chinese Garden commissioned the author to compose the poem "From the Lakeside Terrace of the Lotus Hall," which was published as a broadside to celebrate the garden's fifteenth anniversary in 2015.

Unless otherwise noted, all poems and quotations are those of the author.

I am grateful to Julie Porter and her many students from Portland State University. Your classes have shaped my tours and this book profoundly. And with much gratitude for the series of garden talks given by Cynthia Johnson Haruyama in 2009. I am also deeply indebted to Father Paschal Cheline, OSB (1936-2015), a Benedictine monk of Mt. Angel Abbey, who planted within me a garden of confidence in my talents and abilities.

My thanks to the Lan Su Chinese Garden staff, and to the many garden guests who continually inspire me to dig for new and deeper answers to their questions. I am indebted, as well, to my garden mentor, Lucinda Pierpont. Your knowledge and expertise helped me shape a tour I could call my own. I would also like to give a heartfelt round of applause to Dan Lucas, a gem among gems in this "jewel box in the city."

And finally, my deep appreciation to Ken. Without your love and talent, none of this would be happening.

# ABOUT THE AUTHOR

Daniel Skach-Mills (*Dan Daoren*) has had an affinity with Chinese art and culture since age twelve, when he would use his paper route money to buy Chinese figurines. As an overweight teenager, he was attracted to images of *Pu T'ai*, Daoism's rotund laughing Buddha, whom he frequently turned to for inspiration, solace, and guidance.

Daniel's four books: *The Tao of Now*, *The Hut Beneath the Pine: Tea Poems*, *In This Forest of Monks*, and *Manzou* have all been influenced or inspired by the time he's spent in the garden leading tours and sipping tea. In addition to being published in numerous journals and anthologies, his writings have been used in classes at the University of Minnesota, and in Donald Altman's book, *The Mindfulness Code*.

A former Trappist monk, Daniel considers the garden to be the closest thing to a monastery that he could find in the midst of the city. In this regard, he shares a contemplative kinship with Ji Cheng, the 17th century Chinese author of *The Craft of Gardens* (*Yuanye*), who wrote:

> *If you've found solitude in a noisy place, what need is there*
> *to long for somewhere far from where you live?*

Daniel currently lives with his partner of twenty-five years in Portland, Oregon, where he enjoys writing, playing board games, practicing *taijiquan*, and leading tours at Lan Su Chinese Garden where he has served as a docent since 2005.

# PRIMARY SOURCES

My primary source for this book has been the garden itself. In addition, the following authors and lecturers have been invaluable in rounding out my garden experience.

Adyashanti. *Falling Into Grace: Insights on the End of Suffering*. Sounds True, 2011.

Bartholomew, Terese Tse. *Hidden Meanings in Chinese Art*. San Francisco: Asian Art Museum of San Francisco, 2006.

Cohen, Ken. *Taoism: Essential Teachings of the Way and Its Power*. (CD set) Sounds True, 1998.

Dongchu, Hu. *The Way of the Virtuous: the Influence of Art and Philosophy on Chinese Garden Design*. New World Press, 1991.

Drda, Darrin. *The Four Global Truths: Awakening to the Peril and Promise of Our Times*. Evolver Editions, 2011.

Hardie, Alison, translator. *The Craft of Gardens by Ji Cheng*. Better Link Press, 2012.

Hinton, David, translator. *The Selected Poems of Wang Wei*. New Directions, 2006.

-----------------, translator. *The Selected Poems of T'ao Ch'ien*. Copper Canyon Press, 1993.

Li, June T., editor. *Another World Lies Beyond: Creating Liu Fang Yuan, the Huntington's Chinese Garden*. Huntington Library, 2009.

Macy, Joanna and Anita Barrows, translators/editors. *A Year with Rilke: Daily Readings from the Best of Rainer Maria Rilke*. HarperOne, 2009.

May, Gerald. *The Wisdom of Wilderness: Experiencing the Healing Power of Nature*. HarperCollins, 2006.

Merton, Thomas. *The Way of Chuang Tzu*. New Directions, 1965.

Meyer, Marvin W., translator. *The Secret Teachings of Jesus: Four Gnostic*

*Gospels*. Vintage Books, 1986.

Mitchell, Stephen. *The Second Book of the Tao*. The Penguin Press, 2009.

--------------------. *Tao Te Ching: a New English Version*. Harper Perennial, 1992.

Moeller, Hans-Georg. *Daoism Explained: From the Dream of the Butterfly to the Fishnet Allegory*. Open Court, 2005.

Nepo, Mark. *The Book of Awakening: Having the Life You Want by Being Present to the Life You Have*. Conari Press, 2011.

O' Connor, Mike, translator. *Where the World Does Not Follow: Buddhist China in Picture and Poem*. Wisdom Publications, 2002.

Olson, Raymond. *Blending with Nature: Classical Chinese Gardens in the Suzhou Style*. (DVD) Sacred Mountain Productions, 2007.

Palmer, Martin. *The Kuan Yin Chronicles*. Hampton Roads, 2009.

Sung, Vivien. *Five-fold Happiness: Chinese Concepts of Luck, Prosperity, Longevity, Happiness, and Wealth*. Chronicle Books, 2002.

Tolle, Eckhart. *The Power of Now: a Guide to Spiritual Enlightenment*. New World Library, 1999.

Towler, Solala. *Tales from the Tao: Wisdom of the Taoist Masters*. Duncan Baird, 2007.

Watson, Burton, translator. *Chuang Tzu: Basic Writings*. New York, 1964, 1996.

Watts, Alan. *Tao: The Watercourse Way*. Pantheon, 1975.

---------------. *Taoism: Way Beyond Seeking, the Edited Transcripts*. Tuttle, 1998.

Wong, Eva. *Taoism: a Complete Introduction to the History, Philosophy, and Practice of an Ancient Chinese Spiritual Tradition*. Shambhala, 1997.

Wu, Charles. *Listen to the Fragrance: Literary Inscriptions in Lan Su Yuan, the Portland Classical Chinese Garden*. Portland: The Portland Classical

Chinese Garden, 2006.

Xiaofeng, Fang. *The Great Gardens of China: History, Concepts, Techniques.* Monacelli Press, 2010.

Yang, Jiyu, *The Chinese Scholars' Art.* (DVD) Portland: Dr. Yang's Art Studio, 2013.

# GLOSSARY

**Ba jiao** 芭蕉: ornamental banana plant. Also known as "hardy banana."

**Cha Dao** 茶道: the "Way of Tea."

**Chan** 禪: a syncretism of Daoism and Mahayana Buddhism, which later became Zen in Japan.

**Chashu** 茶樹: camellia sinensis, from which tea is harvested.

**Chiwen** 鴟尾: dragonfish.

**Chuiliu** 垂柳: a willow tree.

**Confucian:** a person who follows the teachings of Kongzi 孔子 (Confucius) which emphasize self-control, adherence to a social hierarchy, and observance of civic rules and protocols as ways to live well and bring order to society.

**Dantian** 丹田: an energy center in the body. There are three *dantian*: the upper *dantian* is located on the crown of the head, the middle *dantian* is in the chest area, and the lower *dantian* is about three inches below the navel.

**Dao** 道: (pronounced "dow." Sometimes spelled "Tao.") means "way" or "path." Although Dao cannot be conceptualized, it is present as the rhythmic, cyclic flow of nature that we witness both around and within us. Awakening to and aligning yourself with this deeper current of life, rather than your egoic mind, is primary in Daoism which de-emphasizes intellectual and academic prowess in favor of intuition, felt experience, and "not-knowing." This "via negativa" (or "negative way" as it is called in the West) is the doorway to a deeper way of knowing. Dao becomes available to our perception when we are aligned with what is happening, rather than our belief in our thoughts about what is happening.

**Daodejing** 道德經: can be translated into English as *Book of the Virtue of the Way*. A manual on the art of governing and living, reputedly written (or compiled from oral sources) by Laozi in the 5th century BCE.

**Daoist:** a person who uses Daoist spiritual practices and principles as a way to live simply and in harmony with the natural course of things.

**Daojia** 道家: the early classical or philosophical form of Daoism (around 500 BCE) usually associated with the writings and teachings of Laozi, Zhuangzi, and Liezi.

**Daojiao** 道教: Daoist religion, which began with the charismatic figure Zhang Daoling, who instituted the Celestial Masters sect along with Daoist clergy in 142 CE.

**Daoren** 道人: "person of the Way."

**De** 得: a Daoist principle which emphasizes bringing forth our unique character and inherent virtue.

**De yi** 得一: "get the meaning or idea."

**Du hua** 讀畫: "Read the Landscape."

**Duilian** 對聯: a poetic couplet.

**Eremitical:** pertaining to the life of a hermit or recluse.

**Erhu** 二胡: a two-stringed Chinese musical instrument played with a bow.

**Feng** 楓: a maple tree.

**Fengshui** 風水: translates as "wind and water." *Fengshui* is the art and science of Chinese geomancy, which focuses on creating the most auspicious energy flow in any given space.

**Fo shou** 福壽: luck and happiness.

**Fu** 蝠: bat.

**Fu** 福: blessing.

**Gongfu** 功夫: "art" or "skill."

**Guan** 觀: building or observatory.

**Gui** 桂花: osmanthus bush.

**Guzheng** 古箏: a Chinese zither that is larger than the *qin*.

**Haitang** 海棠: crab apple.

**Haitong** 海桐: pittosporum, commonly called mock orange.

**Hehua** 荷花: lotus flower.

**Hehuan** 合歡: the silk tree.

**Hulu** 葫蘆: a gourd.

**Jia shan** 假山: an artificial mountain range built of stone.

**Jianzhu** 建築: architecture.

**Jiju** 集句: a word game known as "collaging lines," in which the scholars would challenge each other's literary skill by coming up with poetic couplets.

**Jing** 景: scenery.

**Jinyinhua** 金銀花: winter honeysuckle.

**Jinzhonghua** 金鐘花: yellow forsythia.

**Kongzi** 孔子: Confucius.

**Lamei** 臘梅/蠟梅: wintersweet.

**Lan** 蘭: orchid

**Lan Su Yuan** 蘭蘇園: Garden of Awakening Orchids, the poetic name of Portland Oregon's Chinese garden.

**Langzi** 廊子: covered walkway.

**Laozi** 老子: the Daoist sage who is reputed to have written and/or compiled the *Daodejing*, or *The Book of the Virtue of the Way* in the 5th century BCE.

**Li** 禮: in Confucian philosophy: ritual observance designed to facilitate outward expressions of benevolence and obligation to others.

**Li** 理: originally the Chinese character for the markings in jade. Li is the term for the unrepeatable, organic patterns we see everywhere in human and non-human nature.

**Li Bo [also known as Li Bai]** 李伯/李白: a famous Chinese poet of the Tang dynasty (618-907 CE).

**Liezi** 列子: a philosopher-sage who lived around the 4th century BCE.

**Ling qi** 靈氣: divine energy.

**Lingtai** 靈臺: a tall column erected in the imperial hunting grounds that the ruler would ascend to commune with the deities.

**Liu** 六: the Chinese word for "six."

**Louchuang** 漏窗: tracery leak windows.

**Louge** 樓閣: a two-story building or tower.

**Lu** 祿: prosperity.

**Luoshi** 絡石: star jasmine.

**Mei** 梅: the plum tree.

**Mengzi** 孟子: a Confucian philosopher born in 372 BCE.

**Ming** 明: the Ming dynasty (1368-1644 CE).

**Mudan** 牡丹: tree peony, or peony flower.

**Nanmu** 楠木: a type of wood from the laurel family.

**Penjing** 盆景: "landscape in a pot." *Penjing* are miniature forest and mountain scenes arranged in a tray or pot.

**Pu** 樸: simplicity.

**Qi** 氣: life force energy.

**Qi yun** 氣韻: energy rhythm.

**Qigong** 氣功: a system of rhythmic movements designed for working with one's breath or life energy.

**Qin** 琴: a small Chinese zither.

**Qing** 情: feeling.

**Qing** 清: the Qing dynasty (1644-1911 CE).

**Ren** 仁: in Confucian philosophy: sincerity and benevolence.

**Ren wen** 人文: human culture.

**Ru** 儒: Confucian philosophy.

**Ruixiang** 瑞香: the daphne bush.

**Shan** 山: mountain.

**Shancha** 山茶: camellia japonica.

**Shanmu** 杉木: fir.

**Shanshui** 山水: mountains and rivers, landscape, landscape painting.

**Shi** 石: stone.

**Shige** 詩歌: poetry.

**Shijing** 詩經: *The Classic of Poetry*, compiled in China about 100 BCE.

**Shisun** 石筍: shoot stones, which are tall columnar sedimentary rocks that resemble bamboo shoots.

**Shou** 壽: the Chinese character for long life.

**Shu** 書: book.

**Shui** 水: water.

**Shuixie** 水榭: a waterside building.

**Shuzhai** 書齋: a Chinese scholar's study.

**Song** 松: pine.

**Suihan sanyou** 歲寒三友: the Three Friends of Winter, which are the pine, plum, and bamboo.

**Suo** 鎖: "to lock in."

**Suzhou** 蘇州: Portland, Oregon's sister city, located about fifty miles west of Shanghai.

**Taihua** 太化: the Great Transformation of Things.

**Taihushi** 太湖石: stones from Lake Tai that are used to create mountains in a Chinese garden.

**Taijiquan** 太極拳: (also known as T'ai Chi) a form of exercise characterized by slow rhythmic movements patterned on the movements in nature, especially the flow of water. Based in Chinese medicine, *Taijiquan* optimizes health by keeping the energy pathways (or meridians) in the body open.

**Tang** 堂: a central building or hall in an ancient Chinese home.

**Tang** 唐: the Tang dynasty (618-907 CE).

**Tao Yuanming** 陶淵明: a famous Chinese poet who lived from 365-427 CE. Author of *Peach Blossom Spring*.

**Taohua Yuan** 桃花源: *Peach Blossom Spring*.

**Ting** 亭: a garden pavilion.

**Tingtang** 廳亭: a Great Hall that usually overlooks the largest scenic area in a Chinese garden.

**Wan** 萬: ten thousand.

**Wannianqing** 萬年青: literally "ten-thousand years green," the Chinese common name for the rohdea plant.

**Weiqi** 圍棋: a Chinese board game for two players using black and white stones on a grid of black lines. The object is to surround and so capture your opponent's stones. *Weiqi* translates as "encircling game." Called *go* in Japan.

**Wen** 文: culture.

**Wu** 無: non-being.

**Wu wei** 無為: non-action or not forcing.

**Wu yi** 無意: means "no ideas." Often used as a Daoist admonition to let go of our thinking.

**Wuze** 無則: non-law.

**Xiangqi** 象棋: Chinese chess.

**Xiangsheng** 相生: mutual arising. In Daoist philosophy, mutual arising refers to all things arising together as a unity or totality. Nothing exists by itself separate from everything else.

**Xianqing** 閒情: term for "the good life."

**Xin** 心: heart-mind.

**Xuan** 軒: lounge hall.

**Yang** 陽: the cosmic masculine principle.

**Yi** 義: in Confucian philosophy: justice, duty, and obligation to others.

**Yin** 阴: the cosmic feminine principle.

**Yinxing** 銀杏: gingko wood.

**Yixingni** 宜興泥: purple sand clay used to make *Yixing* teaware.

**Yongquan** 湧泉: the "Bubbling Spring," an acupoint near the ball of the foot.

**Yu** 有: being.

**Yuanye** 園冶: *The Craft of Gardens*, written in the 17th century by Ji Cheng.

**Yuanyou** 園囿: imperial hunting grounds.

**Zen:** see **Chan**

**Zhai** 齋: (a place for) fasting.

**Zhangshu** 樟樹: camphor wood.

**Zhenren** 真人: a Daoist sage.

**Zhi** 智: wisdom.

**Zhiwu** 植物: plants.

**Zhongyong** 中庸: fulcrum, mean, balancing point.

**Zhuangzi** 莊子: a Daoist philosopher who lived during the 3rd century BCE.

**Ziran** 自然: translates as "self ablaze" or "it is so of itself." Used to refer to the self-generative Dao.

**Zisi** 子思: the grandson of Kongzi (Confucius).

Made in the USA
Columbia, SC
27 December 2018